BEAUTIFICATION OF THE BRIDE SERIES

YOU'VE GOT TO HEAR FROM GOD AND IT IS NOT CHEAP

ALEX AMPIAW

xulon PRESS

You've Got To Hear From God And It's Not Cheap
by Alex Ampiaw

Alex Ampiaw
ICCLESIA
P.O. Box 1032 Maumee, OH 43537

Printed in the United States of America

ISBN 978-1-59781-613-7

www.xulonpress.com

CONTENTS

INTRODUCTION

KNOW GOD FOR YOURSELF

> None of them shall teach his neighbor, and none his brother, saying, 'Know the Lord,' for all shall know Me, from the least of them to the greatest of them (Hebrews 8:11).

> For I know whom I have believed (2 Timothy 1:12).

The primary goal of this book is to demonstrate through personal testimonies the reality of God, the truth of His promises and the key to overcoming in every situation. The book reiterates what every person instinctively knows: that God is real. But beyond that, we can each have such a personal encounter with His person and power until we are fully assured that He will honor every promise He makes to us.

The biggest threat to the faith of many Christians is a lack of personal experience with God. It is not sufficient that we merely believe there is a God, because the Bible declares that the demons also believe and tremble (James 2:19). Our faith is solidified when we encounter God in our personal experience, so that our knowledge of Him is not just what someone taught us, but what we know by our own encounter with Him.

God did not just save us from going to hell. His plan of salvation for man goes beyond deliverance from hell. Unfortunately, deliverance from hell is where many Christians have stopped, and have missed the bigger picture in God's heart.

Reconciliation between God and man is the central message of salvation. The sin of Adam caused a separation between man and God; and with that separation came broken fellowship. The plan of salvation is God's remedy to restore that broken fellowship. The message of salvation therefore is: God has forgiven us all, so be reconciled to Him.

The primary motivation behind this reconciliation was God's desire to have a personal relationship with each of his redeemed ones. And because trust is the foundation of any relationship, God is continually refining our trust in him until we come to trust him absolutely. Without this absolute trust, our faith in God and our relationship with Him cannot be complete. Most of the experiences we encounter in life as Christians are, thusly, orchestrated by God to teach us to trust Him and to build up our faith in Him, so that we can know Him better.

Some of these experiences may be very hard and even painful. Although we are inclined to blame every painful experience on the devil, there is nothing in the Bible to suggest that the devil can do whatever he wants to the children of God whenever he pleases without God's purpose in it.

In Isaiah 43:2-3, God says:

> When you pass through the waters, I *will be* with
> you; and through the rivers, they shall not overflow
> you. When you walk through the fire, you shall not be
> burned, nor shall the flame scorch you. For I *am* the
> Lord your God, the Holy One of Israel, your Savior…

God is telling us in the above scripture that sometimes He allows us to go through difficulties or persecutions in order that we may know Him as both our God and Savior. Therefore, any difficult circumstance we face may be an opportunity to receive a deeper revelation of God than what was previously accessible to us.

That this may be the case is actually a great privilege, as we will soon discover that the more we know God, the more we are able to share in His divine nature. When the apostle Paul discovered this revelation, his heart-cry in life became what he summed up in Philippians 3:10: *"that I may know Him..."*

Also difficulties, like a refiner's fire, have a way of bringing to the surface impurities lurking in our heart. As Christians, we often think we love God with all our hearts, and we cannot see that this is far from the truth until He shows us. Jeremiah 17:9 says, *"The heart is deceitful above all things, and desperately wicked: who can know it?"* The fact is, we do not know what is really in our hearts until we face a test that pushes us out of our comfort zone. First Corinthians 11:31 says, *"For if we would judge ourselves, we would not be judged."* Thus, when God allows us to see what is truly in our hearts, He is giving us the opportunity to judge ourselves, so that we may repent accordingly.

Additionally, it is by the relationship we develop with God, through both good and bad experiences of life, that we come to know the ways of God. You see, it is one thing to know for yourself that God is a miracle worker; it is a whole new level to know the principles behind His miracles. Psalms 103:7 tells us that God showed His acts to Israel, but He revealed His ways to Moses. God's ways are the secrets to His power, and He reveals these secrets to only those who have a trust relationship with Him. .

In fact, we cannot have great faith without knowing the ways of God. There is a level of boldness that only becomes accessible when we know the ways of God. The three Hebrew children in the book of Daniel, who were put into the fiery furnace, knew God so well they were able to declare emphatically: *"...our God whom we serve is able to deliver us from the burning fiery furnace, and He will deliver us from your hand, O king"* (Daniel 3:17). It was their knowledge of God's ways that gave the Hebrew children the tremendous faith they needed to stand in the face of an impossible circumstance.

Indeed, those who know the ways of God have greater faith to experience spectacular miracles.

To nurture this kind of faith in us, God takes us through a journey of trials and triumphs until we come to know Him enough to trust Him with our very lives. Faith is so fundamental in the kingdom of God that Hebrews 11:6 says it is impossible to please God without it. Since God is a spirit, it is only by faith that we can relate to Him, and for that matter, anything in the spirit. In fact, just as money is the claim on all material resources in the world, faith is the claim on all resources in the spirit.

The Bible compares faith to gold, and just like gold, faith is more valuable the purer it is. Hence, just as gold is refined by fire to make it purer, so is faith purified through trials (see 1 Peter 1:7 and James 1:3-4). Notice what James 1:4 says about the result we can expect when our faith is purified: *"that you may be perfect and complete, lacking nothing."* This is spiritual prosperity! And it is because of this great gain that accrues to us from going through trials that James 1:2 exhorts us to *"count it all joy"* when we face various trials.

Faith is also defined as being an assurance, according to Hebrews 11:1. It is this assurance that inspires those who have faith to take seemingly ridiculous actions to achieve spectacular results. The lives of Abraham, Moses, David, Daniel and all the rest of the faith giants mentioned in Hebrews chapter 11 give us examples of the quality of trust we can have in God and the kind of results we can expect when we live by faith.

The pertinent question is, how did these people come to acquire this kind of trust in God? We should also wonder how the early Christians were able to maintain their faith in God in the face of cruel adversities. Even when they faced the prospects of the most horrible deaths, they still refused to give up their faith. Was it sheer willpower or mere religious fanaticism? No, I am convinced there was something more to their person than just religious zealotry or tenacity of willpower. Their simple secret was that they knew God for themselves.

This observation is amply supported in the Bible. Read what the apostle John writes in 1 John 1:1-2:

The one who existed from the beginning is the one we have **heard and seen**. We **saw him with our own eyes** and **touched him with our own hands**. He is Jesus Christ, the Word of life. This one who is life from God was shown to us, and we have seen him. And now we testify and announce to you that he is the one who is eternal life. (NLT—emphasis added)

And Peter also gives us the following insight in 2 Peter 1:16-19a:

For we were not making up clever stories when we told you about the power of our Lord Jesus Christ and his coming again. We have **seen his majestic splendor with our own eyes**. And he received honor and glory from God the Father when God's glorious, majestic voice called down from Heaven, "This is my beloved Son; I am fully pleased with him." **We ourselves heard the voice** when we were there with him on the holy mountain. Because of that, we have even greater confidence in the message proclaimed by the prophets... (NLT— emphasis added).

John and Peter plainly show us the source of their confidence. John writes that because they have seen Him with their own eyes and have touched Him with their own hands, they can testify to us that Jesus is the eternal life. Peter says practically the same thing: Because of what they saw with their own eyes and heard with their own ears, they have greater confidence in the Scriptures proclaimed by the prophets of old.

Notice the emphasis on *"with our own eyes"* and *with our own hands*. That was the secret to their undying faith and confidence. Nothing could shake what they had experienced firsthand. And, because of what they had witnessed about God, they all chose to die horrific deaths, refusing to renounce their faith in exchange for their lives. The truth is, these martyrs of Christ did not realize all the promises of God in their lifetime, but they had such a personal experience with God that not even death could shake their trust in Him.

Recent terrorism by Muslim fundamentalists seems to devalue the virtue of dying for one's faith. Followers of Jesus have also died for their faith. But if we listen carefully to the testimonies of John and Peter, who also died for their faith, we will agree that these apostles were not mere fanatics or just living in a fantasy. They were writing about what they had personally seen and experienced.

We should know also that these apostles were victims of the cruelty of others because of their faith, and not the perpetrators of acts of violence themselves, as espoused and practiced by these Muslim fundamentalists. Just as the early Christians faced death gallantly because they valued their relationship with God more than their very lives, we also can face death bravely — death to self and to the world — if we become intimately acquainted with God.

My desire in this book, therefore, is to encourage us to zealously pursue an enduring fellowship with God, and experience God for ourselves. As we become acquainted with God, the Bible will come alive for us, because each principle will reflect our own experiences — not just the experiences of some super-spiritual people that lived in history a long time ago. Each experience with God will also expand our faith, and enable us to reach ever-expanding dimensions of God in whom there are no limits.

Additionally, as we come to understand that the trials that come our way are measured for our growth, our attitude in each trial will shift from why-me pity-parties to a joyous acceptance of these trials. Each trial will be seen as a stepping-stone to a higher level in the spirit and a greater usefulness in the kingdom of God. The devil will look so irrelevant in our experiences that we will start praising God during our trials instead of blaming the devil for them. We will be able to say with the Apostle Paul, *"Therefore I take pleasure in infirmities...for when I am weak, then I am strong"* (2 Corinthians 12:10).

True, knowing God's purpose in a particular adversity will not necessarily lessen our suffering in that adversity, but it will enable us to endure the suffering because of the reward that awaits us on the other side of the adversity. So, whether in trial or triumph, our experience with God is valuable for developing our trust in Him.

We need to remind ourselves, however, that God is bigger than any experience we may encounter in Him, regardless of how great that experience might be. In other words, our experiences, no matter how profound, will never reveal the full breadth of God's character or the full depth of God's wisdom concerning any particular truth.

The Bible declares that God's ways are past finding out (Romans 11:33); and it is my belief that we are going to be discovering God in ever-expanding dimensions throughout eternity. Therefore, the danger is to pitch our tent at one revelation of Him and refuse to believe anything beyond our personal experience.

God reveals His glory to us at a particular time according to the measure of faith we have at that time. As we come to know deeper truths and bear fruits by them, He moves us to another level of faith, and there reveals another level of glory to us. So what we may think is a great revelation at one time may turn out to be only the mere fringes of a deeper truth.

Jesus said it was the job of the Holy Spirit to lead us into all truth. And since the Holy Spirit is the one leading us, He is also the one who orchestrates our circumstances and orders our steps in life. Therefore, let us go through our trials with patience and celebrate our victories with purpose, knowing that all of our experiences are bringing us into a greater knowledge of God and increasing our faith in Him.

The title of this book, *You've Got to Hear from God,* underscores the fact that communication between two parties in a relationship is the life of the relationship. Without mutual communication between related parties, relationships eventually wither. Yet many believers accept a one-way communication with God: they talk to God daily by prayer, praise, and worship, or they zealously read the Bible daily. Only a few expect to actually hear from God and therefore seek to hear from Him.

This book demonstrates that God does speak to us using various media, and He reveals His secrets to those who care for them. Without hearing from God, our relationship with Him will never be complete; our faith will never reach its full strength; and overcoming in every circumstance will be impossible. Therefore, it is imperative that we know the voice of God and seek to hear from Him.

Hearing from God is so precious that one word from His mouth can change the course of our life for good. If we were truly convinced of this truth, how would it affect our desire to hear from God? It is my hope that it will take us only but a few chapters of this book to arrive at the obvious answer to this question.

In teaching me the truths I share in this book, the Holy Spirit sometimes taught me the principles first and then gave me opportunities to experience that truth. Other times, I went through the experience first and then He taught me the principles behind what I had experienced. I have written about some of these experiences or testimonies in the hope that I will be able to demonstrate the workings of the principles behind them in a practical way. It does no good for us to be full of theology or doctrines without understanding how to apply them to our lives.

However, in giving these testimonies, there is a risk that some people may mistake the way these testimonies happened as methods to achieve specific results. Consequently, they may attempt to duplicate the exact manner in which they happened in their own experiences. This is precisely what the message of this book discourages. God is seeking to have a unique personal relationship with each of us, and the way He achieves that goal may be as unique as each one of us.

We have to work out our own salvation with fear and trembling, as Paul instructs us in Philippians 2:12. Search the Scriptures and discover that there are no two miracles recorded that happened exactly the same way. Each believer's faith, and that alone, determines the length, the breadth, and the depth of his or her relationship with God and the blessings that arise out of it. This is what Jesus meant in Matthew 9:29, when He told a person seeking His help, *"Be it done unto you according to your faith."*

My hope is that the principles and experiences discussed in this book will encourage us to put all our trust in God, and to pursue a lifestyle of fellowship with Him until our faith increases to the point that we can say with the apostle Paul, *"I am not ashamed: for I know whom I have believed, and am persuaded that he is able to keep that which I have committed unto him against that day"* (2 Timothy 1:12).

CHAPTER 1

THE REALITY OF GOD

Anyone who comes to God must believe that he is
real. —Hebrews 11:6 *ICB*.

Believe me when I say that I am in the Father and the
Father is in me. Or believe because of the miracles I
have done" —John 14:11 *ICB*

The Dead Are Raised

I used to be both skeptical and curious, an unkindly mix of
personal qualities that cost me great opportunities and led me
into many fruitless adventures. But God would deal with my skepticism and use my curiosity in a most unusual way to bring me into
His kingdom; and the story I am about to tell was the beginning of
several unique experiences that God employed to establish my faith
in Him.

It began on a Tuesday morning—not a favorite day or time for
typical church activity, much less, a day to expect a great miracle.
Nevertheless, on this fateful day I found myself in a small church,
having been invited by friends who for months had been enticing

me with incredible stories of miracles regularly taking place in their church. I remember being in the midst of fifteen to twenty anxious people praying fervently to receive the baptism of the Holy Spirit.

I do not believe I had truly given my life to Christ at this time, but I was familiar with the concept of the baptism of the Holy Spirit, having attended a Pentecostal church during my childhood. After a man fervently preached and convinced us of the absolute necessity of receiving this gift of God, I plunged into what I believed was an earnest prayer to receive the Holy Spirit.

The leaders of that particular Tuesday meeting, however, were on a holy assignment, and I discovered after a while that no one was going to leave that meeting without the Holy Spirit. These leaders were more eager to get me baptized in the Holy Spirit than God Himself! I felt fire and brimstone all around me. One man actually put his mouth on my ear screaming something to the effect that if I do not receive the baptism of the Holy Spirit, I could not make it to heaven. Immediately, my skepticism surrendered to fear. I shifted gears from earnest prayer to frantic begging.

After what seemed to me a frightfully long time without anyone receiving the Holy Spirit, my fears gave way to frustration. My frustration soon yielded to wandering thoughts, and with them, my skepticism crept back with a vengeance. The realization that I still had not received this all-important gift from God made me afraid. My continual failure to receive this gift made me even more frustrated, more unfocused and more skeptical. I was despondent. Several times, I stopped to peek through one eye to see what was going on with rest of the seekers. I do not remember the expressions on their faces, but I am certain they were all as tired as I was. Or perhaps they were too over-zealous to see the barrenness of our effort, as we pressed on relentlessly in prayer.

Then, suddenly, God had mercy on me! No, I did not receive the baptism of the Holy Spirit with the evidence of speaking in tongues, as we had been led to anticipate. I know no one else did either. What I mean is that something interrupted the zealous flow in the room. The sudden silence was so deafening, I opened my eyes to see what was the matter. A few of the men rushed out and, after a space of time, returned carrying a woman. She had died in her house, and some of

16

her household members believed they could get a miracle from the church, so they rushed her to the church. But, by the time they brought her, she was stone dead and so stiff they had to prop up her body to keep her from rolling off the bench on which they had laid her.

Now, growing up in a Pentecostal church, I saw many strange things happen in the church, enough to make me religious, and more than enough to make me dread the thought of giving my life to Jesus. I witnessed experiences such as 'falling under the power', praying in tongues, and dancing in the Spirit—all of which caused me great discomfort. I also listened to several bizarre testimonies that often appeared to give more glory to the devil than to God.

But, there on that fateful Tuesday, I was about to witness one of the most daring of these spiritual experiences. The lead person (who I later learned was not the pastor, as I had imagined) called us to gather around the dead woman, and charged us to pray for her to come back to life.

After the Holy Spirit nightmare, I had added to my skepticism a religious fear. If I was going to Hell because I did not have the Holy Spirit, I was not about to worsen my life in Hell by questioning the sanity of these church people. In plain language, I thought they were crazy, but I was too scared to disclose my opinion.

Well, if they were counting on *my* prayer for that woman to come back to life, then I must have been the sole reason she didn't after a long time of prayer. Half of the time, I just stared with bewilderment at the earnestness in their faces, as they prayed with all their might. They really prayed like they expected the woman to come back to life through their prayers.

Then the fervency of the prayers began to wane, as most of them got tired or lost hope for success. Eventually the prayer ceased altogether. What I did not know was that they had sent for the senior pastor of the church to come and help. He appeared in the doorway, walking slowly towards us, seemingly unperturbed by the emergency at hand. He stopped at where the exasperated leaders were standing and rebuked them for not being able to raise the lady back to life.

That was where my curiosity kicked into gear. Who was this man so confident that he actually thought his church members ought to have been able to raise a dead person? He directed that the body be laid on two benches, and as one of the men reached out to keep the body from falling off, the pastor restrained him, saying that there were angels holding the woman, and that she would not fall. Miraculously, without any support, the dead body did not fall off the benches!

At that instance, I was no longer skeptical, only curious to know what this pastor was going to do to raise the woman up. What kind of incantations or prayers was he going to say? After touching the lady on the head and on the feet with his walking stick, he prayed about two sentences and shouted, "In Jesus Name!"

That was all it took. The lifeless body began to shake. The woman opened her eyes momentarily and fell back dead again. The pastor touched her again and shouted the same phrase, "In Jesus Name!" The woman stirred up for the second time and opened her eyes; and this time, she remained fully conscious. Her hands were still stiff from rigor mortis. The pastor held her hands and repeated the same phrase again, and instantly, her hands were loosened. He took her hand and helped her to stand up. He then gave her to her husband, who was an elder of the church and had been praying with us earlier. As the three of them walked out of the church, I overheard the pastor rebuking the husband for something he had done and warning him not to let that happen again.

What happened to the rest of my quest for the Holy Spirit on that Tuesday morning is now irrelevant, even if I could remember it. The reason I am writing about this incident is to show how that miracle impacted my faith from that day forward. From that day, I very much wanted to know God. I knew for a fact God did work miracles. Years of skepticism about all those who claim to have had a miracle dissolved under the weight of one mighty act of God's sovereignty.

This miracle so impacted my life that, later, when I gave my life to Christ, I could not be satisfied with Christianity as usual. I pursued God with all my heart until I began to experience God's power for myself, as I describe throughout this book.

It is too late to tell me that miracles are not real, or they were needed only in Bible times when the church was in its infancy and other such theological mumbo-jumbo. My prayer for you is that, as you truly become acquainted with God, your own life will be similarly impacted.

However, I do not tell this story to imply that all or any of our experiences with God will necessarily be this dramatic. I made the point in the introductory chapter that what we experience in God will be as unique to our faith and calling as God chooses. What I meant to establish here was that God is real, and that there is more to His kingdom than what today's lukewarm Christianity suggests.

I believe God invites us to explore all the depths of His riches in Jesus Christ. Notice that all the people who received commendations from Jesus for their faith dared to believe beyond the obvious. (See, for examples, the centurion and the Syro-Phoenician woman in Matthew 8:5-13 and Luke 7:24-29 respectively.) Therefore, we should never settle for average Christianity, when there is so much more inheritance to possess in Jesus.

For me, God chose the path of the miraculous to break my unhealthy skepticism and to forge in me an unyielding trust in Him. The path He takes each person may be different, influenced only by how far that person is willing to trust Him with his or her life.

Whenever I tell this story, peoples' attention is, understandably, drawn to the miracle of raising the dead back to life. But the crucial question in the story for me is, why was this pastor of a small local church so sure God would raise the dead woman? He rebuked his assistants for their failure even before he did anything about the situation, implying there was no question in his mind that the woman would live again. What was the source of this pastor's boldness in the face of a seemingly impossible situation?

The obvious answer is, of course, his faith. But how could anyone acquire such tremendous faith? The not-so-obvious answer is that this pastor knew God on a different level than his assistants did. We could assume that it was having this level of knowledge about God that gave David the boldness to slay Goliath (see 1 Samuel 17). In fact, we can re-list all the other faith giants in Hebrews chapter 11 for this same quality: they all knew God so well, and trusted Him to such a degree that the fear of death lost its grip on them.

Within a few weeks after this amazing incident, God made sure every trace of unbelief about the reality of His power was erased from my mind. I attended a mass crusade conducted by a well-known American evangelist and witnessed several other notable miracles. The most spectacular of these was in regard to a young man of about twenty-five years who was crippled from birth. This man stood up and walked on his own two feet for the first time in his life. The stunned expression of sheer ecstasy that lit up his face was the proof of authenticity of this miracle, even as his over-joyous family further testified on his behalf.

And here again, it was not the miracles per se that got my attention. It was the evangelist's simple message and prayer that produced such incredible miracles that got me wondering. From that time on, I was hooked on God. He is real and He works miracles! All my skepticism was gone for good, replaced by a deep hunger for the things of God. My curiosity remained, but now, it was redirected to explore the hidden riches of Christ.

Even so, the answer to my burning question continued to elude me for some time: How did these men of God obtain so much grace and faith to perform such incredible feats? The following chapters explore some of the answers I have now come to understand through experience and by direct revelation from the Holy Spirit, even as my quest to know God more intimately continues unabated.

CHAPTER 2

THE MASTER KEY TO ALL PROMBLEMS

Problems that Seem to Defy Prayer

Have you ever faced a situation that seemed to defy all remedies? You have prayed all kinds of prayers and made all the faith confessions you know, yet nothing has changed so far. One preacher said, if you increased your giving, your problem would go away. So you gave your best offering with great expectation, but nothing changed. Another preacher said, you needed to target your seed when you give; therefore, you gave a sizeable amount in offering, targeted specifically for that particular need. Yet it has been a while, and you have not seen any results. Later, you came to learn that praise and worship were the keys you were missing; and there you went, praising God with all your heart, and yet the victory for your kind of issue has remained elusive. In other words, you have applied all the principles you have been taught, but your situation remains unchanged.

Many of us as Christians have one or two problems like that in our lives, and once in a while, we wonder why we don't get a breakthrough for a particular persistent problem. Other Christians, however, are too religious to admit that somehow their prayers failed to get the answers they sought. Somewhere in their religious training, someone taught them that questioning why their prayer failed to produce results amounted to unbelief. So they continue to hang on to a hope that may never materialize.

Often we are perplexed when we read the Bible, because the promises of God appear so within reach in our imagination, and yet they seem so far away in our daily experiences. For instance, Jesus said, *"Ask, and it will be given to you; seek, and you will find; knock, and it will be opened to you. For everyone who asks receives"* (Matthew 7:7-8). And again he said, *"If you have faith as a mustard seed, you will say to this mountain, 'Move from here to there,' and it will move; and nothing will be impossible for you" (Matthew 17:20)*. When we consider the simplicity of these Scriptures, we begin to feel as if we can move heaven and earth with our faith. Nevertheless, victory continues to elude us, in spite of our super-charged faith.

If you do have a situation like that and feel despondent about it, you are not alone because the disciples of Jesus had similar disappointments. After one of those moments of disappointment, as recorded in Matthew 17:19, they came privately to Jesus and whispered to him, *"Why could we not cast it out?"* Let me take the liberty to paraphrase their question to Jesus: "Lord, we applied all the faith we had; why were we not successful?" I know they were really confused when Jesus answered, *"because of your unbelief"*, and then added,

> If you have faith as a mustard seed, you will say to
> this mountain, 'Move from here to there,' and it will
> move; and nothing will be impossible for you (v. 20)

Faith (as little) *as a mustard seed!* The disciples must have had some faith for them to even attempt to heal the boy; so what was Jesus trying to teach them? He was trying to get them to the root of their failure, which could be found in his next statement to them: *"However, **this kind** does not go out except by prayer and fasting"* (v. 21).

I am aware that different people interpret this Scripture differently. Some believe *"this kind"* refers to the demon the disciples could not cast out; and others believe it refers to the disciples' unbelief. I do not intend to join the debate, but I believe the correct interpretation is obvious from the question the disciples asked Jesus.

Regardless of how it is interpreted, however, Jesus was revealing to the disciples that fasting and prayer was the key to victory in the situation they confronted. In other words, they needed a different kind of faith to deal with that *kind* of problem — a specific strategy to win that specific battle; and that fasting and prayer would have endowed them with the necessary equipment or wisdom to get victory.

Most of the situations that defy solutions in a believer's life can qualify for the *'this-kind'* exception. Unfortunately, our immaturity or sheer laziness prevents us from accessing the right solutions for our problems

The point is, there is an answer to every legitimate prayer; there is a key to each difficult situation; and there is a strategy for victory in every battle. These statements may surprise some people, and may evoke cynicism in others who have been defeated so many times they are afraid to trust God again for a breakthrough. Such people have abandoned themselves to mediocre faith, coasting through their Christian lives, expecting nothing beyond the ordinary, and deferring all their hopes to a "sweet by and by" in Heaven.

But hear me, a major reason for this book is to assure those who are sincerely seeking God that there is a sure way to win every battle. I mean every single battle! God has repeatedly revealed the way to us in the Bible.

I know some well-meaning people will be quick to point out all the prayers that have gone unanswered in so many circumstances. I also know that Paul asked three times to be rid of an infirmity, and got a not-so-clear answer from God. But even here, notice that Paul did not stop praying until he got a response from God (see 2 Corinthians 12:8-9).

I reassert that there is a sure way to win every battle. However, sometimes, winning the battle is not necessarily getting the exact results we had expected, as was the case in Paul's example above.

Understanding God's Purpose in Trials

We must understand that virtually every trial that shows up at our door was sent or allowed by the Holy Spirit for our training, reproof or promotion. So what at times appears as attacks of the enemy may actually be the hand of God accomplishing a specific purpose in us. In that case, the answer to a besetting problem is not for the problem to go away, but that we allow it to produce the effect God wants to achieve in our lives.

To be able to respond appropriately regarding a particular difficulty in life, however, requires wisdom and discernment from the Holy Spirit. This is one reason why we have to have an ear to hear from God.

James 1:2 reads in part, *"Count it all joy when you fall into various trials"*. But, in order for us to maintain our joy when we go through a trial, we have to be able to know that God authorized the particular trial we are dealing with. And we must also know how to conduct ourselves in that difficult time. This is why verse 5 of the same Scripture instructs us to ask God for wisdom regarding the trial we are facing. The following is my own testimony regarding this subject.

I was in the middle of a battle that had the potential to alter the course of the rest of my life. Without first seeking the mind of God about the issue, I concluded that this was a battle sent from hell to ruin my life. And so I plunged into prayer warfare trying to defend and salvage everything I could. But the more I fought, the worse the situation got. All my prayer to God was for Him to make the problem go away. And it did not; it only grew worse.

Then I remembered James 1:2, and realized that I had not asked God for wisdom regarding the situation. So I asked Him for wisdom. Well, the answer was unexpected but, suddenly, I began to appreciate that this particular problem was a blessing in disguise. Instead of the pain and grief I initially felt about the issue, I now began to see some of the benefits this painful experience could bring to my life.

Even with this revelation, I still felt the anxiety of having to change for an uncertain future. Nevertheless, my knowledge of God's purpose in the situation made my discomfort bearable and welcomed. Thus, James 1:2 is encouraging us to be joyful in trials because, through those trials, God is achieving His purpose in us, which is to bring us to a position of full spiritual prosperity (see v. 4).

In fact, it is because of the prosperity that accrues to us when we endure afflictions that we are exhorted in 1 Peter 5:8-9 to resist Satan during our time of suffering:

> Be sober, be vigilant; because your adversary the devil walks about like a roaring lion, seeking whom he may devour. *Resist him, steadfast in the faith*, knowing that the same sufferings are experienced by your brotherhood in the world (emphasis added.)

There is an apparent paradox or irony in play regarding the above scripture in the light of James 1:2. On one hand, we are exhorted to be joyful in a trial because of the benefit it brings. On the other hand, in our trial, we are instructed to resist Satan, the very instrument of this beneficial trial. Is there a contradiction here? Not at all! Even though God may allow Satan to buffet us sometimes (as in the cases of Job – Job 1:12 and Paul – 2 Corinthians 12:7), God's objectives in trials are never the same as Satan's.

We have already understood that God's purpose in trials is to bring the believer to a position of greater spiritual prosperity. But the ultimate goal of the enemy in all trials is always harmful, and it is three-fold: to steal, to kill and to destroy (see John 10:10). Satan uses the suffering that comes with trials to discourage the child of God and to discredit the integrity of God —"if God loves you so much, why does He allow all these bad things to happen to you" is the taunting of the enemy during the afflictions of the child of God.

It is this discouragement we are to guard against as believers, lest we lose faith and stagger in unbelief. It is the issue of our faith that is at stake here, because it is our faith that enables God to accomplish His purpose in us. And it is by our faith that we can endure adversity and quench the fiery darts of the enemy.

The only time Satan succeeds in his objective is when we lose faith and get discouraged. This is why the exhortation in 1 Peter 5:8-9 makes sense in the light of James 1:2. In fact, rejoicing in a trial is part of our weapons of resistance against Satan's discouragement, *"for the joy of the Lord is your strength" (Nehemiah 8:10).*

The story of Job exemplifies the above explanation. We know that Job's afflictions came from Satan; but we also know that it was God who permitted Satan to afflict Job. In his pain, Job moaned, complained and argued, but never once did he lose his faith in God. Job's summary attitude in all his afflictions is captured in the following two Scriptures:

> But He knows the way that I take; when He has tested me, I shall come forth as gold (Job 23:10).

> But as for me, I know that my Redeemer lives, and that he will stand upon the earth at last. And after my body has decayed, yet in my body I will see God! I will see him for myself. Yes, I will see him with my own eyes. I am overwhelmed at the thought (Job 19:25-27—NLT)!

Hence, we see in Job's example how the enemy sought to destroy him through discouragement, and we see how Job resisted him steadfast in the faith. And what was God's purpose in all this? That Job will come into full prosperity, both spiritually and physically.

We shall revisit God's purpose in Job's story at a later chapter, but the point is well made at this juncture that our faith is of utmost importance at all times, whether we are on top of the mountain or at the bottom of the valley of life experiences.

Pumping Our Faith Muscles Through Trials and Triumphs

The foregoing explanation leads us to a rhetorical question: if God is working His purpose in us through the adversities we face in life, why then should we seek to overcome the adversity we are facing? The Bible says the afflictions we face as believers are producing for us an immeasurable amount of glory (see 1 Corinthians 4:17). So why should we expect God, who allowed the adversity in the first place, to answer our prayer for deliverance from the adversity?

The answer to this second paradox is in the fact that God does not merely allow us to go through adversities to see who can endure the most pain, as if the pain itself is the qualifier for spiritual progress. That would be spiritual torture! No, adversities are like weights in a gym. They stretch our faith muscles to tone them for beauty and greater strength. The suffering or pain we experience is simply the byproduct of the stretching of our faith muscles.

Let us carry the gym analogy a little further. In the gym there are several pieces of equipment to tone different muscles in the body. So in order to have a complete workout for all your muscles, you have to move from one piece of equipment to another. Thus, in our faith experience, we face *diverse* temptations or trials to help us to be complete, lacking nothing. Is not this exactly what James 1:2-4 says?

With this understanding in mind, we conclude that no adversity should be permanent in our life. Paul describes adversities as momentary light afflictions (see 1 Corinthians 4:17). Therefore, we should be overcoming and moving on from faith to faith and from glory to glory (see Romans 1:17 and 1 Corinthians 3:18).

Overcoming the particular adversity besetting each of us at any time, therefore, is a path to greater fruitfulness in the kingdom of God. We have to know that God sees us as more than conquerors (see Romans 8:37) because Christ has already overcome on our behalf. Therefore, we ought to approach each adversity that comes our way with a mindset of victory.

If God has preordained victory for us in every adversity, then we can rest assured that He has also provided a key to victory in each situation. This is why God gave us the following promises to encourage us to seek His face for the keys we need to unlock our victories:

> Ask, and it will be given to you; seek, and you will
> find; knock, and it will be opened to you. For everyone
> who asks receives, and he who seeks finds, and to
> him who knocks it will be opened. Or what man is
> there among you who, if his son asks for bread, will
> give him a stone? Or if he asks for a fish, will he give

him a serpent? If you then, being evil, know how to give good gifts to your children, how much more will your Father who is in Heaven give good things to those who ask Him (Matthew 7:7-11.)

And whatever things you ask in prayer, believing, you will receive (Matthew 21:22.)

...Most assuredly, I say to you, whatever you ask the Father in My name He will give you. Until now you have asked nothing in My name. Ask, and you will receive, that your joy may be full (John 16:23b, 24.) If you can believe, all things are possible to him who believes (Mark 9:23.)

The only condition attached to these promises is the faith needed to do what these Scriptures say. Most promises in the Bible carry conditions for their fulfillment, as we will discuss in Chapter Five. But the ones shown above do not. God is big enough to give us an unconditional promise and to fulfill it when a demand is made on it. It is a *carte blanche*, but who has the faith to take God up on his word?

What we typically do is disguise our unbelief by coming up with our own conditions. We believe there has to be a condition, and finding none, we make one up on our own, usually a very difficult one to allow us a good excuse for failing to get answers.

There is one condition for anything in the kingdom of God and that is our faith — faith to believe that God means exactly what he says and says exactly what he means. The spiritual walk is delicate enough without us complicating it with our own rules and conditions.

I am aware of the fact that God only hears us when we pray according to His will (see 1 John 5:14.) But the question here is why do some problems remain unresponsive to prayer even though we know it is God's will for us to have a breakthrough?

Again let us examine one of the most powerful promises Jesus made to believers:

> Have faith in God. For assuredly, I say to you, whoever says to this mountain, 'Be removed and be cast into the sea,' and does not doubt in his heart, but believes that those things he says will be done, he will have whatever he says. Therefore I say to you, whatever things you ask when you pray, believe that you receive them, and you will have them (Mark 11:22-24—NLT).

Whoever and *whatever* mean exactly what they say. And here again, there was no condition except to *"Have faith in God."*

However, sometimes we sincerely believe we have faith, and yet we still do not get answers to certain prayers. The logical question that arises then is, did God have a hidden condition when He made promises like the ones above, or is there something wrong with our faith? We will explore how God's promises are meant to be exactly what they say and how we can have success each time.

My prayer is that each one of us will discover the rich inheritance God has bestowed on us in Christ Jesus and be able to live the victorious life that God has designed for each one of His children. If we discover and appropriate this heritage, our very lives will become the gospel by which God will attract the world unto Himself. This goal is what is implied in Isaiah 60:1-3:

> Arise, shine; for your light has come and the glory of the Lord is risen upon you...the Lord will rise over you and His glory will be seen upon you. The Gentiles shall come to your light and kings to the brightness of your rising.

To that end, God is equipping His people to become what Paul describes in 2 Corinthians 3:2 as an *"epistle... known and read by all men."* Yes, we are being equipped to demonstrate the glory of God not by mere words but by our exemplary lives. In these last days, keys to hidden treasures of the kingdom of God are being released to whoever has an ear to hear what the Spirit is saying. Seals to secrets that have been kept intact throughout the ages are being broken for release to all who would prove themselves qualified. And below is the master key that unlocks these incredible treasures of God to us, and enables us to overcome every adversity in our lives.

The Master Key: The Word that Proceeds Out of the Mouth of God

Several years ago, the Holy Spirit began to show me the key to receiving answers to every prayer. He also granted me the privilege of experiencing the workings of this key in other situations and, thereby, affirming its immutability. Consequently, I have come to believe that every promise of God in the Bible is true, and most of them are achievable right now in this life. I truly believe that you can have whatever you say, and nothing will be impossible to you if you have faith as Jesus promised.

However, getting to this level of faith is not cheap, because it demands a higher level of knowledge of God. Do not be disappointed for this requirement; you will soon appreciate why this is so.

Another primary objective of this book, therefore, is to show the reader the necessity of acquiring this higher knowledge of God and the awesome rewards awaiting those who press on to possess its privileges. The following testimony began the journey that culminated in the writing of this book.

A Revelation From Satan!

My best friend was very ill. He had a severe stomach ulcer that often attacked with such ferocity that it would leave him writhing in pain on the floor for a long time. For weeks, nothing would heal it. He went through several prayer lines of some of God's most anointed preachers we knew at the time; and just when he thought he had finally obtained his deliverance, the pain would suddenly return with awful consequences. All medications he tried gave him only a temporary relief. And so this on-and-off condition continued for several days.

One day, while on a visit at my house with other friends, his stomach ordeal came upon him without warning. He appeared to be in so much pain that we immediately gathered around him to pray. We prayed fervently for some time without apparent results. Then, suddenly, the Holy Spirit drew my attention to a Scripture in Luke 4. It was the Scripture about Jesus being tempted in the wilderness. In that Scripture Satan in a scheme to cause Jesus to act out of self-will made this rather harmless statement: *"If you are the Son of God command this stone to become bread"* (Luke 4:3).

This Scripture has nothing to do with healing, so why would the Holy Spirit show it to me in the middle of an emergency in need of a healing virtue? As I was wondering about the Scripture, the Holy Spirit began to show me how Satan recognized the authority of the Son of God and acknowledged that the Son of God had power in his command. Therefore, the key was: if we believed we were also sons of God, we should stop praying and command the sickness to go in the authority of the Son of God.

Faith indeed comes by hearing the word of God! I stopped the prayers immediately, and told my other friends what I had just heard from the Holy Ghost. So we stretched our hands towards him and commanded the sickness to leave his body. And immediately, the pain stopped! All it took was about 30 seconds. And more importantly, my friend did not experience another attack of the pain after that breakthrough.

Did you get the revelation in this? It is not the letter of the Scriptures memorized by rote and regurgitated by heart that has the power. It is rather the word that *proceeds* out of the mouth of God that produces life. I had always known the Scripture in Luke 4:3, but when the Holy Spirit quickened it in my spirit, it came alive with power.

This is what many have referred to as the *spoken* word or *rhema* (in the Greek) as opposed to the *written* word or *logos*. It is the word proceeding from the mouth of God. This is the word God wants us to live by daily as He declares in Deuteronomy 8:3.

The letter of the Scriptures will do nothing for us except make us religious unless the Holy Spirit opens our spiritual ears to hear what He is saying to us in the Scriptures. This, I believe, is the essence of what Jesus said in John 6:63: *"It is the Spirit who gives life; the flesh profits nothing. The words I speak to you are spirit, and they are life."*

I could not have imagined the Scripture in Luke 4:3 as a weapon of choice for the miracle we needed for my friend's sickness, because it had nothing to do with healing. In my limited understanding, the authoritative Scripture for healing was Isaiah 53:5, and as affirmed in 1 Peter 2:24: *"And by His stripes we are healed."* But this Scripture primarily establishes the legal basis for us to expect healing when we pray for healing. In other words, as believers, we are entitled to expect healing when we pray because Christ has already paid for our healing. However, the wisdom for a particular sickness at a particular time may not necessarily be Isaiah 53:5, but may be something else quite unexpected.

All of God's word is health to man, as declared in Proverbs 4:22; and depending on the situation at hand, the Holy Spirit may send the particular word needed for that specific situation. The question is whether we have an ear to hear what the Spirit is saying to us about our peculiar problems?

My faith was different after my friend's miraculous healing. I will stake my life on this: if you hear God speak and you act on it by faith, you shall have whatsoever you pray for. And here is the reason:

> For as the rain comes down, and the snow from
> Heaven, and do not return there, but water the earth,
> and make it bring forth and bud, that it may give seed
> to the sower and bread to the eater, so shall My word
> be that goes forth from My mouth; It shall not return
> to Me void, but it shall accomplish what I please, and
> it shall prosper in the thing for which I sent it (Isaiah
> 55:10-11).

Yes, the word that proceeds out of the mouth of God *shall* accomplish the purpose for which it was sent.

We have more to say about Isaiah 55:10-11 throughout this book, but I learned several things from my experience. I began to understand why our prayers are sometimes barren of results in spite of all the assurances Jesus gave us. That day, I could also relate intimately with the Scripture that we quote so often: *"Faith comes by hearing and hearing by the word of God" (Romans 10:17.)* However, the greatest lesson I learned was that there is a strategy for every battle, and knowledge of what to do in each specific instance will get victory each time.

In this particular testimony I just described, the solution did not depend on volume of intercession, or even fasting and prayer, as Jesus had revealed in the case of the epileptic in Matthew 17. Neither did it depend on faith confession of the promises of God. The key was simply to command the sickness to go in the authority of the Son of God.

Notice the different methods Jesus used in his healing ministry. Sometimes he just spoke a word and the sick were healed; one time he mixed clay with his spit and smeared it on a blind man's eyes. In the case of the ten lepers, he simply told them to go show themselves to the High Priest, and as they went, they received their healing.

Interestingly, Jesus had this great success without ever stopping to pray to the Father before he healed the sick. He merely spoke to the problem and it was gone. In only one instance, before he raised Lazarus (John 11:41, 42), he thanked the Father for hearing him, but he quickly added that he gave thanks for the benefit of the people around him.

Why did Jesus not pray to the father to achieve results? It was not necessary. He had such close fellowship and constant communion with the Father that he knew exactly what to do each time. In his own words: *"...the Son can do nothing of Himself, but what He sees the Father do; for whatever He does, the Son also does in like manner"* and again, *"As I hear I judge..."* *(John 5:19b, 30).*

Most of the great miracles recorded in the Bible occurred because someone heard and obeyed the word of God. I believe this is the key to great victories in prayer. For us also to be effective ministers of God in the world, we have to walk by the voice of God. Two problems may look alike on the surface but the underlying cause may be dramatically different in each case. That is why we need God's wisdom in every situation; and this is why we have to hear from God to be successful every time.

Many times we pray hoping that God will answer someday, and if we do not see results after a long period, we let our expectations slide into oblivion, assuming that our quest was not the will of God. The Bible says that God hears us if we pray according to his will, so if we know the will of God in a situation, we should by all means pray that will. But if we are not sure what to do, then our first action in prayer is to seek God's will about the matter. This is especially critical in praying for another person's deliverance from demonic oppression. We must know what we are dealing with before we attempt to do warfare against the powers of bondage.

The Only Lawful Language in the Spirit

When we deal in the spirit, we are dealing in legalities, and we better have a solid legal basis for issuing commands. Because everything is subject to the word of God, whatever word God sends us regarding a situation becomes the legal basis for demanding compliance in the spirit. The word of God is the only language the demons understand and submit to. Remember Satan's words, *"If you are the Son of God, command..."* Who is the Son of God? *"For as many as are led by the Spirit of God, these are sons of God"* *(Romans 8:14).*

Anyone who is born again and has the Holy Spirit dwelling in him or her has the right to claim the title, *son of God* (John 1:12). However, the authority of the son of God is fully manifested in only those who hear and move by the word of God. This is what Jesus showed us through his example: *"As I hear I judge..."* Satan recognizes the authority vested in the sons of God, because the authority of the son comes from the Father (see John 5:22–27).

We shall explore this truth further in succeeding chapters. But listen to Lamentations 3:37: *"Who is he that speaks and it comes to pass when the Lord has not commanded it?"* We had better believe this Scripture! This is why sometimes we pray issuing commands and decrees and yet we see very little results. The only thing firmly established in Heaven is the word of God. The only thing that will never pass away is the word of God. And listen to John 1:3 where the word of God is personified in Christ, *"Without the Word was nothing made that was made."*

James 5:17-18 says that *"Elijah was a man with a nature like ours, and he prayed earnestly that it would not rain; and it did not rain on the land for three years and six months. And he prayed again, and the Heaven gave rain, and the earth produced its fruit."* The immediate understanding that comes from reading this Scripture is that Elijah's prayer could do incredible things, even though he was as human as we are. What is not readily apparent is the fact that those prayers were not made out of self-will. Elijah prayed in accordance with the will of God for that occasion, and that was why his prayer was answered.

How do we know this was exactly the case? Three main reasons: We just saw the first reason in Lamentations 3:17, which states that no one can speak anything into existence when God has not ordained it to be so. Secondly, 1 John 5:14 says that God only hears us if we pray according to His will, and God was no different in Elijah's day than when John wrote that Scripture. But here is the ultimate proof from Elijah's own mouth, when he was praying for fire to fall from Heaven during his challenge with the priests of Baal in 1 Kings 18. Verse 36 of that chapter reads in part:

> ...Lord God of Abraham, Isaac, and Israel, let it be known this day that You are God in Israel and I am Your servant, and that *I have done all these things **at Your word*** (emphasis added).

What does *"all these things"* refer to? It applies to all the events that took place at the word of Elijah, from 1 Kings 17 through the slaying of the prophets of Baal in 1 Kings 18:40.

Are you now beginning to see why much prayer and faith confessions among Christians never bear any fruits? The biggest cliché among the Charismatic movement for a long time was, *"confession brings possession"*. There is a lot of truth in that statement, but if that were the whole truth, then most Christians, especially Charismatics, would be super wealthy by now. I still have confessions dating back in time that are yet to see the light of day, and I know you may have quite a few unanswered ones yourself. If God is not slack concerning His promises (see 2 Peter 3:9), why are some of His promises taking forever to manifest? Well, do not hold your breath because they may never materialize because of Lamentations 3:17.

Do not misinterpret what is being said here. This is not to establish a doctrine for all unanswered prayers. Answers to some legitimate prayers may take time to manifest because of other reasons, and we will examine some of those reasons in subsequent chapters. The legitimacy of our confessions is the issue at stake here and not the timing of answers to prayer.

Confession that brings 'possession' is not the result of cherry-picking Scriptures from the bible and throwing them back at God. Satan also tried the same trick when he was tempting Christ in the wilderness. His favorite cloak of deception was: *"it is written"*, as he quoted the Scriptures and threw them at Christ. And what was Christ's first response? *"It is written, 'Man shall not live by bread alone, but by every word that **proceeds from the mouth** of God'"* (Matthew 4:4).

If we want to achieve God's results, then we must be saying the same thing God is saying. This is the *spirit of faith* mentioned in 2 Corinthians 4:13:

> And since we have the same spirit of faith, according to what is written, 'I believed and therefore I spoke,' we also believe and therefore speak.

This is also the spirit of prophetic utterances:

> For prophecy never came by the will of man, but holy men of God spoke *as they were* moved by the Holy Spirit (2 Peter 1:21).

And this was, therefore, the spirit behind Ezekiel's prophecy regarding the valley of dry bones in Ezekiel 37:7): *"So I prophesied as I was commanded…"*

We are the echo of the voice of God in the earth; we are the Amen of His word in the earth. God speaks from Heaven; our agreement with the spoken word and our action in line with that word establishes the will and purposes of God in the earth. We were created in the image of God to *represent* Him on earth, and not to *replace* Him. Ecclesiastics 12:13 sums up the whole duty of man on earth: to obey God.

We will see in Chapter 10 why *obedience* is such a good thing for the child of God, and why God insists on it so strongly. So we should be seeking out the will of God and establishing it in the earth instead of following our own ambitions and desires. This is the only way we can bring the blessings of Heaven into the earth.

We will discover in Chapter 7 that God has already spoken or is yet speaking what His will is for us. However, the real challenge is hearing what He is saying. That is why He wants us to give our undivided attention to what He is saying to us; and He minces no words about the issue. He speaks to us through His Son in Luke 8:18:

> So be sure to pay attention to what you hear. To those who are open to my teaching, more understanding will be given. But to those who are not listening, even what they think they have will be taken away from them—NLT.

This statement implies that, as believers, our victory is directly proportional to our understanding of God's will and to our actions in accordance with that will.

We will expound more on this truth in succeeding chapters. For now, it is sufficient to say that your stubborn problem may be in need of the proceeding word of God. The following testimony demonstrates once again how powerful this truth is.

The Case of the Unstable Pregnancies

I have seen a certain incidence happen too many times in the church. A person is prayed for, and immediately testifies about being healed of an infirmity. But we see the same person in the prayer line with the same condition not many days after. Is it because the healing was not real, or is it because the person opened the door again to whatever used to hold him captive.

When Jesus healed the man who had been plagued with an infirmity for thirty-eight years, he told him to go and sin no more lest a worst thing come upon him (John 5:1-8). We can infer from Jesus' warning to this paralytic that a person could get sick again after being healed, if that person went back and did whatever gave the devil the legal basis to afflict him or her in the first place. I do not believe Jesus meant that we have to lead perfect lives to receive or maintain our healing from God. If that was the case, then no one could qualify for a miracle. What that statement simply suggests is that some afflictions are the results of sins in a person's life.

The pertinent question is, how can a cancerous condition vanish from a person's body and instantly return after a few days? The answer is, unless it did not really go away in the first place. In medical circles there is a phenomenon called the *placebo effect*. This often occurs in volunteers who are subjects in a test for a new drug.

For instance, volunteers for the test may be divided into two groups. One group receives the real drug being tested and the other half is made to believe they are also taking the real drug but are given instead a phony drug called a placebo that does absolutely nothing. The key is both groups of volunteers believe they were given the test drug.

It has been found that some of the subjects given the placebo actually report feeling better after taking the phony medicine. One reason for this is the fact that much of the feelings of well-being and the feelings of indisposition have to do with the state of mind we are in. If we believe we are well, we feel well; if we believe we are sick, we actually feel sick even though, physiologically, nothing has changed in our body.

The point is, many people in need of healing are often caught up in the euphoria of the moment, and actually feel better after being prayed for; therefore, they presume they have received a miracle. That is nice but not good enough. *"If the Son makes you free, you shall be free indeed" (John 8:36)* is the wonderful truth about divine healing. It is true you need faith to maintain your healing, because Satan will come to test the word that was the basis of your healing. But you have to move into total unbelief to really lose what God gave you by grace.

There is such a thing as total healing or total deliverance in the kingdom of God. Moses told the Israelites *"For the Egyptians whom you see today, you shall see again no more forever" (Exodus 14:13).* The Israelites were taken into captivity by several pagan nations none of which was bondage in Egypt again.

I can testify that this is true, as I have personally experienced such complete deliverance from a particular affliction that used to plague me in the past. After my healing, I lived in what some would describe as divine health for nearly seven years without suffering a single episode of infirmity of any kind whatsoever (including fatigue, headaches or colds.)

Let me get on with my story. I am a member of the intercessory group in our church and a leader over one of the several teams within the intercessory ministry. A young lady on my team at the time had several pregnancies terminated mid-term in spite of all the prayers on her behalf and her own unwavering faith. I can testify that this lady was so full of faith and hope that she wholeheartedly believed each particular pregnancy was going to be successful. But not long after she gave her testimony of how God had blessed her with another pregnancy she would miscarry again. Nothing would weaken this lady's faith, however. And there she was again and again, testifying after each new pregnancy. I truly admired that woman's faith and persistence.

But one day, I decided enough was enough, and started asking the Holy Spirit for the key to this woman's condition. I knew a lot of people were praying for her situation; therefore, I did not think one more prayer by another person was going to get the job done. Rather, I was asking the Holy Spirit to reveal a specific word or strategy that would unlock the solution for the lady's condition.

It was not her persistent testimonies that bothered me but rather what appeared to be a mockery of the devil. The devil would wait long enough for her to believe a particular pregnancy was going to stay. Then soon after she gave glory to God, she would miscarry the baby.

I did not immediately receive any specific direction from the Holy Spirit after my prayer. Every month, intercessors in our church are assigned specific personal spiritual exercises they must do individually. In one particular month, we were not assigned any special assignment; but each intercessor was encouraged to ask the Holy Spirit for direction about what to do for that month. As I knelt down to pray for direction, the Holy Spirit said: "Pray in the spirit for two hours each day for the next three days for the lady with the aborting pregnancy" (I am paraphrasing). This was the key I had been waiting for.

As a prayer warrior, I am used to praying in the spirit regularly, but this particular assignment proved to be one of the toughest I had ever engaged in. It was not tough just for the two hours of unceasing prayer in the Spirit, but rather all the things the devil did to prevent me from accomplishing the task.

At the end of the three days, I went and told the woman that she would not miscarry on her next pregnancy, and that I would show her the reason for my confidence after she delivers her baby. You see, that was not a prophecy I received from the Lord. I was just confessing by faith what I believed was the key to her victory, based on what the Holy Spirit had taught me over and over again: that the word from God's mouth acted on by faith will *never* fail to produce the results expected.

Well, the woman got pregnant again, and this time it remained for the entire term. As I write, the woman has had two more children to add to her miracle. Of course, I am not claiming my prayer alone was responsible for her miracle, as many people had been praying for her situation. But I can say with all certainty that the woman's situation turned on the word I heard from the Holy Spirit and acted on by faith.

This concept of the 'proceeding word' is remarkably powerful in the kingdom of God. Everything in the universe is subject to the word of God, because everything was created by the word of God. Yet, we often take the word of God for granted, and neglect to give it the priority it merits in our daily lives. Therefore, in the next chapter, we present an in-depth understanding of why God's word is so powerful. Perhaps this will help cure apathy towards the single most important thing in the entire universe: the word that proceeds out of the mouth of God.

CHAPTER 3

THE SUPREMACY OF THE WORD OF GOD

You have magnified Your word above all Your name"
(Psalm 138:2).

Forever, Oh Lord Your word is settled in Heaven
(Psalm 119:89).

My covenant I will not break, nor alter the word that
has gone out My lips (Psalm 89:34).

But the word of the Lord endures forever (1 Peter
1:25).

Every Christian ought to understand this fundamental truth: the
word that proceeds out of the mouth of God is the biggest thing
in the universe. Therefore, it is absolutely necessary for a person
seeking to have a closer walk with God to be able to know His voice.
This is not an option in spiritual life. And the Bible is very plain
about the fact that our ability to follow Jesus depends on our capacity
to hear his voice, as John 10:4 declares: *"...The sheep follow Him,*

for they know His voice." Again, in John 10:27: *"My sheep hear My voice...and they follow Me"* And in Romans 8:14 we read: *"For as many as are led by the Spirit of God, these are sons of God."* But the Spirit of God can only lead us effectively if we can hear His voice. We will get into the subject matter of *spiritual hearing* later; but we need to establish the point that hearing from God is the key to a fruitful spiritual life in God. And the following sections explain why.

The Word of God is the Essence of God Himself

The word of God is God revealing Himself, His purposes, His plans and His principles to man. It represents the mindset of the invisible God; therefore, God's word is His very essence. So, when John 1:1 reveals Jesus to be the Word of God, it also reveals that the Word was God himself.

This understanding is critically important, because it implies that any word out of God's mouth carries the full power of God behind it. It also implies that God and His word are inseparable. If this is true, then it will not be an overstatement to say that God will do nothing without his word. In fact, this is exactly what verse 3 of John 1 says: *"...Without Him (the Word) was nothing made that was made"* — Nothing in the universe was made without the word of God!

The fact that the word of God represents His very essence should not surprise us, because not only is God invisible, but there is nothing in the universe that can adequately represent Him. He told Moses that no man could see His face and live. By implication, if God were to reveal himself physically, His form would be incomprehensible to man. Any attempt to represent God by any image will only serve to limit our notion of Him to whatever qualities that image inspires in our imagination. This is one of the main reasons God commanded the Israelites not to make any image to represent Him.

Because God cannot be represented by anything in the universe, He manifests His presence by His word. This disposition of God toward man is not the result of the fall of Adam. The Bible mentions that Adam and Eve heard the *voice of God* walking in the Garden of Eden, and they hid themselves from the *presence of God* (see Genesis 3:8 — KJV).

The voice of God, by implication, indicated the presence of God. Any interpretation of the Scripture beyond this, no matter how fascinating, would be mere speculation. Therefore, the interpretation we should assign to Genesis 4:16, where it is stated that Cain went out from the presence of the Lord, is that Cain never heard the voice of God again from that time forward.

Nothing Exists Outside of the Word of God

The foregoing section leads us to a rhetorical question: If God himself will do nothing without His word, why would He approve of us doing anything without His word? In fact, He does not only disapprove, but it is impossible for anything to exist outside of the word of God. Why? Because the entire universe was created, functions and is held in place by the word of God. According to Hebrews 1:3, God upholds *all* things by the word of His power. Hence, it is imperative that we get this point engraved in our understanding: Nothing in the universe exists outside of the word of God.

Even evil exists because of the word of God. If not, how can we reconcile 1 John 1:5 and Lamentations 3:38? First John 1:5 states that *"God is light, and in Him is no darkness at all"* (KJV). But then, in Lamentations 3:38, we are surprised to read: *"Out of the mouth of the Most High proceedeth not evil and good" (KJV)*? How can evil proceed out of the mouth of God in whom is *"no darkness at all"?* The answer is *evil* and *good* are the two sides of the same coin. When God speaks, the same word is both a blessing and a curse. Obedience to the word releases the blessing and disobedience releases the curse.

Also consider the following in Psalm 139:7, 8, and 12:

> "...Where can I flee from Your presence? *If I make my bed in Hell, behold, You are there*...Indeed, the darkness shall not hide from You ...The darkness and the light are both alike to You" (emphasis added)

The above Scripture is saying that, nothing in the universe is outside the realm of God, good or bad. As we have already explained, it is the voice of God that demonstrates His presence. And Psalm 139 reinforces that notion, revealing that not even Hell is outside of the realm of God's word.

The Word Activates the Power of God

The fact that the word of God is the reason for everything in the universe is worth belaboring, because it is the foundation for success or failure in all our Christian experiences. Everything exists because of the word of God; and everything is held together by that same word. And hear this: by the same word, the heavens and the earth as we know them will pass away.

Additionally, God's power is released through His word. In Hebrews 1:3 we read:

> Who being the brightness of His glory and the express image of His person, and upholding all things by *the word of His power...*

"The word of His power"! Did you get that? God's power is communicated or activated by His word. And it is this powerful word that sustains the entire universe according to Hebrews 1:3.

Now, let us learn from God as He creates our world. Virtually every creative act of God in Genesis Chapter 1 was preceded by the phrase: *"... God said."* He first made a declaration, and then He acted in accordance with the spoken word.

For instance, Genesis 1:6-7 we read: *"Then God said, 'Let there be a firmament in the midst of the waters and let it divide the waters... Thus God made the firmament and divided the waters...';* verses 14-16: *"Then God said, "Let there be lights in the firmament..."* *"Then God made two great lights..."*; And in verses 26 and 27: *"Let us make man in our own image ...So God created man in His own image."* So we see that, in each creative instance, God said what He was about to do and then proceeded to do it.

Why did not God simply proceed to do what he was about to do but spoke out his intention first? After all, He is God, and could do just that. The answer to that question has tremendous impact on kingdom life and the believer's accomplishments. It was the *declaration*—the *speaking*—of the word that released the power of God to accomplish

His purpose. Remember what we just said about Hebrews 1:3? In speaking forth, God is releasing the *word of His power*.

This is the reason God places so much significance on our words, our tongue and our confession in the Bible. And we will do well to heed Jesus' warning in Matthew 12:36:

> But I say to you that for every idle word men may speak, they will give account of it in the day of judgment. For by your words you will be justified, and by your words you will be condemned.

Also in Proverbs 18:21 we are warned: *"Death and life are in the power of the tongue and those who love it will eat its fruits."* Thus, it is plain that power is released through words.

This was the revelation the centurion mentioned in Matthew 8:8 received. He accurately discerned the vehicle of Christ's power when he said, *"...Only **speak a word** and my servant will be healed."* He recognized that it was not the physical presence of Jesus per se that activated his power but his word, just as the centurion's own words influenced his subordinates to take action. Jesus marveled at the centurion's understanding of such a deep spiritual principle.

God Sustains Us by His Word

The preeminence of the word of God was the first lesson God taught the people of Israel after He had redeemed them from Egypt. Moses echoes this in Deuteronomy 8:3:

> So He humbled you, allowed you to **hunger**, and fed you with manna which you did not know nor did your fathers know, that He might make you know that man shall not live by bread alone; but man lives by every word that proceeds from the mouth of the LORD.

Perhaps, some may overlook the desperation the Israelites were facing in the wilderness, when they started crying to God for food and water. It would be scary enough to find yourself in the middle of a desert without food or water. But imagine a whole nation, between two to three million people, in a desert area with no food and water.

The desperation of the Israelites was legitimate given their predicament. If God did not intervene, they would face certain death. But that was exactly the effect God wanted to produce in them. The question then is, why would God deliberately walk Israel into such hopelessness?

Up until the time of their exodus from Egypt, all that Israel had was a history and a promise that had been handed down from past generations. All of this history led to a man: Father Abraham. The God of Abraham was their God only because they were descendants of Abraham. They did not know God for themselves.

Exodus 9:16 reveals God's reasons for all the plagues He brought upon Egypt and the incredible deliverance of the Israelites from the hands of Pharaoh. Speaking to Pharaoh, God said: *"But indeed for this purpose I have raised you up, that I may show My power in you, and that My name may be declared in all the earth"* *(Exodus 9:16).* Hence, the great display of power God exhibited through Moses was God's way of introducing Himself as the ELOHIM—the Sovereign and Supremely Powerful God—the God of Abraham, who the Israelites had heard about all through their history until then.

Regrettably, after all those miracles, all the Israelites could see was Moses, the great prophet who could perform greater magic than Pharaoh's magicians. Remember how quickly they turned to idol worship as soon as Moses was out of their sight (see Exodus 32.) The God of Abraham had now become the God of Moses to them. Therefore, God had to do something to shift their faith from Moses to Himself. He had to confront them with a dire situation that no man, no matter how great a magician he was, could resolve.

The Israelites had come to believe that Moses could work great magic, like bringing plagues upon the Egyptians and opening the Red Sea. But what magic could feed more than a million people in a desert area? That was something no flesh-and-blood magician could accomplish. It had to be God. So in bringing the Israelites to a point of desperation, God set the stage to reveal Himself to Israel as, EL SHADDAI—the All-Sufficient One— their only source of provision (and not Moses.) They were about to find out for sure that the God of Abraham was also their God, and He was sufficient for all of their needs.

See how God began to shift their attention from Moses to Himself: In Exodus 16, Moses repeatedly reminds the people that their complaints were against God and not him. Then Moses promises them that God would manifest His glory to them, and would send them food and meat every day. The very next morning God appears in His glory, and says to them:

> I have heard the complaints of the children of Israel. Speak to them, saying, 'At twilight you shall eat meat, and in the morning you shall be filled with bread. **And you shall know that I am the LORD your God'** (v. 12).

We quote the above Scripture to demonstrate that God's main goal in bringing the people to the point of despondency was so they would know He was the LORD their God. Notice that God purposefully did not send food that they were familiar with. They had no earthly concept for what He sent them, so they named it *manna,* which means, "What is this?"

God used the manna as a metaphor to accomplish two things: First, His word was food just as good as the regular food they were accustomed to. Therefore, if they were hungry, all they would need was a word from God. Secondly, food that was not of this world taught them that the miracle could only have come from God, not Moses.

According to Romans 15:4, *"whatever things were written before were written for our learning."* Therefore we would do well to learn this first lesson: that our well-being depends entirely on the word that proceeds out of the mouth of God. God teaches us this lesson by leading us through various life circumstances that challenge us with needs. God does not want us to search for solutions anywhere else, but from Him alone. To the degree we seek to discover our own solutions through our own wisdom, He waits until we run out of options and turn to Him.

Jesus taught us to pray, *"Give us this day our daily bread"* (Matthew 6:11) to emphasize this truth. We are called upon to depend on God for our daily sustenance. Pay particular attention to the phrases, *this day* and *daily bread*. They reveal to us that God has determined a portion of bread for us each day. This bread is His word; and He wants us to seek it and live by it daily.

The Messianic prophecy in Isaiah 50:4 shows how Christ's daily dependence on the word of God would enable Him to accomplish His mission on earth: *"He awakens Me **morning by morning**, He awakens My ear **To hear** as the learned."* This was how Christ accomplished a great ministry in his time. He did not succeed merely because He was the Son of God, but because He depended solely on the proceeding word of God.

The fall of Adam and the temptation of Jesus in the wilderness were about the same principle of dependence on the word of God. We know how Adam failed. So let us see how Jesus, on the other hand, overcame the tempter. We saw the ultimate goal of Satan in this temptation in the previous chapter. But now let us examine more closely some of the finer points of Satan's deception:

Jesus was hungry after forty days of fasting. The natural thing for him to do was to get something to eat. Then come Satan to him, approaching him from the most obvious point of weakness, which was Jesus' need for food at the time. Satan's aim was to exploit the weakness of Adam—if Jesus will also seek to depend on Himself for His sustenance. It was not the mere act of eating food that Satan was after. That act by itself would not have been wrong. Satan was enticing Jesus to use his self-will to produce sustenance for himself.

We can see through the subtlety of Satan's deception in his encounter with Jesus when we consider the following two Scriptures:

"Faith comes by hearing the word of God" (Romans 10:17).

"Everything that does not come from faith is sin" (Romans 14:23—NIV).

Do you see the trap? If Jesus acted without the word of God, he would be operating outside of faith, and Romans 14:23 says an action that is not the result of faith is sin. So Jesus would have sinned by commanding the stones to be changed into bread, when God had not spoken to Him to do so.

Furthermore, by obeying Satan's word, Jesus would have been subject to Satan through the same principle that Adam lost his authority to Satan, as we shall briefly explain in the next section. Jesus had to pass this test; else he would go down the same path of failure as Adam did. But Jesus sees through the deception: he does not eat of the fruit of the tree of the knowledge of good and evil. He is moved only by the proceeding word of God.

At the risk of overemphasis, we repeat that Jesus' complete dependence on God for his sustenance was the secret to his extraordinary power and success. Listen to his own testimonies: *"I say to you, the Son can do nothing of Himself, but what He sees the Father do; for whatever He does, the Son also does in like manner" (John 5:19). "I can of myself do nothing. As I hear, I judge..." (John 5:30). "...The words that I speak to you I do not speak on my own authority..." (John 14:10).* So if Jesus depended on the word of God all the time for his success, why do we think we can depend on God only part of the time and still expect good results?

In Proverbs 3:5, we are commanded, *"Do not lean on your own understanding, in ALL your WAYS acknowledge him..."* Failure to acknowledge God in all our ways is the biggest reason many Christians are unfulfilled in regard to the abundant life Jesus promised believers.

Jesus gave a parable to teach us that men ought to pray always and not faint (Luke 18:1-8). Praying always means depending on God always. This is not the place to show the importance of prayer in the believer's life; but it is enough to say that prayer is the demonstration of our dependence on God.

The Oneness of the Word of God

We discussed in an earlier section that the word of God birthed everything in the universe, as recorded in the first chapter of Genesis. Every time God spoke, the word unleashed a momentum of power by which action taken in accordance with the spoken word produced the result or blessing intended. On the other hand, if an action taken was contrary to God's word, a negative result ensued. This negative result is what we call, a curse.

The same word that said Adam could eat of every tree in the garden (Genesis 2:16) also said, *"But of the tree of the knowledge of good and evil you shall not eat"* (v. 17). Accordingly, by choosing to disobey a portion of God's word, Adam disobeys the whole word of God.

We have shown how the word of God is the essence of God himself; therefore, partial obedience to any word of God is still disobedience to God. This principle of *oneness* of the word of God is laid out in James 2:10-11:

> For whoever shall keep the whole law, and yet stumble in one point, he is guilty of all. For He who said, "Do not commit adultery," also said, "Do not murder." Now if you do not commit adultery, but you do murder, you have become a transgressor of the law.

What does all this mean? The curse that God pronounced on Adam and Eve, when they sinned, was not God cursing them out of bitterness or disappointment. God was merely declaring to them the consequence of their choice.

By Lamentations 3:38, we have understood that both "good and evil" or "blessing and cursing" are the opposite sides of the same coin. Since the word of God upholds everything in the universe, no action in the universe can be neutral of the word of God. Therefore, rejecting the blessing of the word is, at the same time, choosing the curse of the word.

Adam's dominion over the earth was similarly birthed by the word of God: *"Let us make man...and let them have dominion..."* Therefore, Adam's ability to dominate also depended on his harmonious relationship with the word of God. So by choosing to disobey the word of God, Adam instantly loses his connection to the authority to rule the earth. Henceforth, achieving dominion in the earth would not come without his sweat and toil, as God revealed in declaring the curse upon him.

The authority to dominate the earth passes on to Satan by another spiritual principle we casually mentioned in the previous section, and which we will do well to learn. Romans 6:16 states this principle very clearly:

> Do you not know that to whom you present yourselves slaves to obey, you are that one's slaves whom you obey...?

Adam obeys Satan; Adam becomes Satan's slave and, immediately, Adam's authority also becomes the property of Satan. Satan acquires the legitimate right to administer the earth instead of man. That was why in Luke 4:5-6, we read:

> Then the devil, taking Him up on a high mountain, showed Him all the kingdoms of the world in a moment of time. And the devil said to Him, "*All this authority* I will give You, and their glory; *for this has been delivered to me*, and I give it to whomever I wish (emphasis added).

We know God did not give Satan *authority* over this earth; but Jesus did not dispute Satan's claim because of the principle in Roman 6:16 above. Adam *delivered* it to him; therefore, Satan was able to legitimately offer Christ the kingdoms of the world and their wealth. It is not mere speculation, therefore, to suggest that Satan, through unbelievers, controls the larger portion of the wealth of this planet simply because of this reason.

Of course, this authority has returned to man through Christ's death and resurrection. As knowledge of spiritual authority increases, believers will be able to access more and more of the wealth of this earth. By the end of the age, believers will experience the fullness of this authority and the glory associated with it. And the prophecy that *"the wealth of the sinner is laid up for the just"* (Proverbs 13:22) will be fully realized.

The Word of God Initiated the Principle of Authority in the Earth

The subject of authority in spiritual life is so important that it is necessary for us to lay some foundations here if we are to understand our need to seek God for His word. Many endowed men of God have written more expertly about this subject in the past. What I present here is to simply emphasize the point that God stamped everything He created with His authority. The following relates specifically to the initiation of the principle of authority in the earth in the beginning.

We have already established the fact that God's word activates His power. We extend this notion to say that God's word is His authority. There were three commands of God relating to man's creation and his authority on earth in Genesis Chapter One.

1. *"Let us make man in Our image after our likeness."* (Genesis 1:26). When God said, *"Let us"*, He was commanding Himself, just as He commanded everything He created to appear or to reproduce after itself. In commanding Himself, God was also subjecting Himself under the authority of His word. This meant that God could not violate His own word, even if He wanted to.

    Additionally, by creating man in His own image, God established a unique relationship with man. He endowed man with His image and likeness to give man the capacity to relate to Him in all aspects of spiritual life.

2. *"Let them have dominion... over all the earth"* (Genesis 1:26). This established the relationship of man with the earth, and subjected the earth to man. Therefore, as it is with man, so it is with the planet. This is the reason the earth was subjected to futility when Adam and Eve fell (see Romans 8:20-22 and Genesis 3:17b)

3. *"Of the tree of the knowledge of good and evil you shall not eat"* (Genesis 2:17). This established God's authority over man. It made man a steward of God, and therefore, account-

able to the word of God. For it is impossible for anything to exist outside of God's authority.

We see that in all three statements, God is defining authority in the earth; and by including Himself under His own authority, God creates an irrevocable principle where authority is elevated as the highest principle in the universe. That is why in Psalm 138:2, we read: *"You have magnified Your word above all Your name" (KJV).* By implication, God has magnified His authority above all His name, considering that God's word represents His authority.

Consequences of Adam's Rejection of God's Authority

Much has been written about the consequence of Adam's fall. We ourselves have experienced, and are surrounded everyday by the corruption that was the result of the fall. Therefore, it would be superfluous to do an in-depth discussion of the subject at this time. What we present here is to merely demonstrate the connection of this corruption to the word of God, which we also defined to be God's authority.

The word of God was the life-source of Adam and Eve. The command, *"Let us create man in Our image…"* (Genesis 1:26), was the source of their existence. In the new birth experience, it is no different. The word of God is still our source of existence, because, according to 1 Peter 1:23, we are born again by the incorruptible word of God.

Therefore, as soon as Adam and Eve disobeyed the word of God, they were disconnected from their life source; and they died instantly. Their immediate death was a spiritual one—separation from God's life—which ultimately led to the cessation of their physical life. This was demonstrated in their losing spiritual consciousness, and becoming self or soul-conscious after they had eaten the forbidden fruit. That was the first lesson God gave man: "Everything is connected and upheld by my word. In the day you disobey me, you will disconnect from your life source, and you will experience death."

It is hard for some people to see the severity of Adam's choice, because they are so much distracted by the symbolism used in the story of the fall. They cannot see how the mere eating of a fruit, forbidden or not, could result in such dire consequence for all men. But the story of Adam is not about a fruit. Nor is it even about a simple disobedience to God. Adam's action was tantamount to high treason. In fact, it is the same sin Lucifer committed that caused him to be booted out of Heaven.

In defense of the truth, let us digress a little to highlight some of the issues in the story of Adam's fall. Here is the general picture of Satan's scheme to deceive Eve:

> Then the serpent said to the woman, you will not surely die. For God knows that in the day you eat of it your eyes will be opened and you will be like God, knowing good and evil (Genesis 3:4).

"You will not surely die…"! This was saying God lied to them. And, *"…You will be like God, knowing good and evil"* also implied they did not need God to make moral choices for them. In other words, they could live independent of God, and still be successful. *"To be like God"*, reflects the age-long desire of Satan that cost him his position in Heaven, as revealed in Isaiah 14:13-15:

> For you have said in your heart: 'I will ascend into Heaven, I will exalt my throne above the stars of God; I will also sit on the mount of the congregation; On the farthest sides of the north; I will ascend above the heights of the clouds, *I will be like the Most High.*' Yet you shall be brought down to Sheol, to the lowest depths of the Pit.

Notice that Satan said so many things in his heart, but as soon as he imagined in his heart, *"I will be like the Most High"*, he received a reaction from God in verse 15, *"Yet you shall be brought down to Sheol, to the lowest depths of the Pit."*

Why did Satan's desire to be like the Most High immediately prompt a reaction from God? The answer is, because there cannot be two sources of authority in the universe. This is an impossibility, the very thought of which violates God's sovereignty. Declaring to

You've Got To Hear From God And It's Not Cheap

be like the "Most High", amounted to declaring to be independent of God's authority. Without delving into the theology of the subject, we simply reemphasize here that authority is the highest principle in the universe, and all of it flows from one source— God.

The concept of one God or the oneness of God derives from this principle of authority. Hence, even before the first commandment, to love the Lord with all their heart, was read to Israel, Moses' declaration to them was: *"Hear, O Israel: The LORD our God is **one** LORD"* (Deuteronomy 6:4 - KJV).

The point is, Adam and Eve fell into the same deception as Lucifer. God subjected all things He created to Himself, and then subjected Himself to His own word. That is why the word of God is supreme, and nothing in the universe can exist outside of it.

Therefore, any authority (appropriately, delegated authority) that presumes to operate outside of the word of God is illegitimate, and will ultimately be crushed. So when Satan tempted Adam and Eve with the possibility of becoming *like the Most High*, he was aiming them at the sin that he knew God would not forgive—a competing authority in the earth.

But Satan's scheme was not merely to spite God by causing the loss of His most prized creation. Satan was still pursuing his old desire to have a world all to himself, where he would be worshipped just *like the Most High*. He knew if he could get Adam to choose self-determination, Adam would become like God having his own authority to make moral laws.

Hence, by exploiting the spiritual principle of obedience and slavery, as we learned earlier in this chapter, Satan would become the owner of Adam's authority and the god of this new world—the world as we see it today. Satan obtained his wish, even if temporarily.

Nevertheless, there cannot be two sources of authority in the universe. This is the reason for the *Day of the Lord*, as prophesied throughout the Scriptures. The *Day* when God will bring judgment upon all who oppose His authority, and establish the oneness of His authority for all eternity. This notion explains 1 Corinthians 15:24-28:

After that the end will come, when he will turn the Kingdom over to God the Father, having put down all enemies of every kind. For Christ must reign until he humbles all his enemies beneath his feet. And the last enemy to be destroyed is death. For the Scriptures say, "God has given him authority over all things." (Of course, when it says "authority over all things," it does not include God himself, who gave Christ his authority.) Then, when he has conquered all things, the Son will present himself to God, *so that God, who gave his Son authority over all things, will be utterly supreme over everything everywhere* —NLT (emphasis added).

The ultimate goal of the restitution of all things mentioned in Acts 3:21 is that *"God...will be utterly supreme over everything everywhere."*

Remember what Christ said after His resurrection: that all authority was given unto him (Matthew 28:18). This was the same authority Adam lost to Satan. God is able to entrust to Jesus all authority because, as the *Last* Adam, he had proven himself faithful.

Unlike the *first* Adam, Jesus is administering this authority on behalf of the Father until he puts all God's enemies (those asserting competing authorities) under his feet. Then the faithful Son will subject himself unto the Father, so that the Father will be all in all.

Thus, Adam deserved the consequences he received, just as Satan received his just penalty to live in Hell for all eternity. The difference between Satan and Adam was that Satan, as an angel and a servant of God, did not have the privilege of choosing his own destiny as Adam had. Therefore, there was no plan of redemption for Satan. Thus, Satan is lost forever.

On the other hand, for man's privilege of choice to be meaningful, there must necessarily be an accommodation for him to make wrong choices. Since the privilege of choice implies the possibility of making a wrong choice, God made provision for man's salvation in anticipation of such a possibility. That is why the Bible declares

Christ to have been slain from the foundation of the world (see Revelation 13:8). Even before Adam showed up, there was a plan to save him from the possibility of his fall.

Nevertheless, it is important to remember this crucial point: that any action independent of God's authority will not survive God's Day of Judgment. This is why mere good works can never make any man right with God. Anything initiated of man's self-will is of the tree of the knowledge of good and evil.

Notice that even the *good* of the forbidden tree of knowledge is still contrary to God's will. This has implications for our faith walk, and influences our success or failure as Christians. We will therefore examine in greater detail this tree of the knowledge of good and evil in the next chapter.

The Impotence of Satan

Before we go any further, however, let us dismantle one of the greatest misconceptions about Satan. Let us begin by saying that Satan has absolutely *no* authority on earth in this present age. Mark my words carefully; I did not say he does not have any *power*. The confusion between *power* and *authority* in the mind of the believer is what the devil has exploited to deceive many.

When Adam yielded to the deception of Satan in the garden, he literally became a slave of Satan, as we deduced earlier in this chapter. The universal principle governing slavery, as we learned, was that whatever a slave has, including offspring and property, belongs to his master. This was the principle Satan exploited in the Garden of Eden.

We also learned that Satan did not cause Adam to fall merely to spite God. No, he was too selfish for that. Satan was still pursuing the one desire that caused him to fall out of his Heavenly position: to *"be like the Most High"* (see Isaiah 14:14)—to be worshipped as God.

But he had no legitimate kingdom to demand worship. God had punished Satan's rebellion by casting him into utter darkness and emptiness, suspended between Heaven and earth with no real estate in the universe. I believe that is why he is referred to as the *"the prince of the power of the air"* (Ephesians 2:2). That punishment was the biggest blow to the over-bloated ego of Satan. How could he receive worship when he had no real estate, no kingdom and no subjects? But he was not called Lucifer for nothing. He would find a way, seemingly, to thwart the plan of God.

He knew God had given Adam the earth, as the Bible affirms in Psalm 115:16: *"The Heaven, even the Heavens, are the Lord's; But the earth He has given to the children of men."* He also knew God's word was law and, therefore, if he could trick the man to obey him instead of God, the man would become his slave and, with that, everything God had given him. Satan would gain legal authority to rule the earth as God had commanded Adam. Satan succeeded in his scheme, and that became the basis for his claim in Luke 4:5-6: *"All this authority I will give you, and their glory; for this has been delivered to me, and I give it to whomever I wish."*

We have already understood why Jesus did not challenge Satan's claim, because that was exactly what happened in the Garden of Eden. Adam handed over the administration of the earth to Satan by obeying him.

Now also is evident the three-pronged strategy of Satan in the temptation of Jesus. All three were disguised as serving different purposes but the truth is they all had one aim: to make Jesus obey him. When Satan said "change these stones into bread," it had nothing to do with bread and stone but about obedience. When he said "cast yourself down from this tower," it had nothing to do with suicide but again to get Jesus to obey him. When he said "worship me," it was all about getting Jesus to obey him. Notice that Jesus' response was also to emphasize the same thing. When Jesus replied each time with *"it is written"*, he was making it clear he obeyed only the word of God.

Jesus, the Last Adam, passed the test this time around. So Jesus was able to tell his disciples in John 14:30, *"The ruler of this world is coming and he has nothing in me."* That is, Satan had no claim to anything that belonged to Jesus. Jesus had not obeyed Satan in the least; therefore, he had no ownership of him.

But Jesus' obedience alone could not free mankind from the penalty of the sin of the first Adam. That sin must be atoned for because of the following principles: *the wages of sin is death (Romans 6:23); the soul that sins must die (Ezekiel 18:4b); without the shedding of blood there is no remission of sin (Hebrews 9:22).* Jesus must die in order to release mankind from the legitimate claim of Satan over man's inheritance, and to satisfy the justice of God.

In death, Jesus entered Hell and spoiled Satan of all the authority he gained from Adam. So, when Jesus was resurrected, he was able to say *"All authority has been given to me in Heaven and on earth"* (Matthew 28:18). *"All authority"* means all authority, and with that statement, Jesus effectively proclaimed the end of Satan's authority on earth and over man. But just as he was free then in the Garden of Eden to deceive and defraud, so now he is walking about in the earth seeking whom he may devour! He is empowered only in so far as someone obeys him.

Now if Satan has absolutely no authority on earth except what man allows him, then you can see how it is possible to succeed every time and not experience even a single defeat. This is true! There is a place in the Christian walk where Satan cannot touch you legally. There is a boundary beyond which Satan cannot cross. This is the same boundary that kept him from touching Job until God took it away to fulfill His purpose in Job (see Job 1:9-10.)

So Satan entices believers to cross over to his side through disobedience to God. The Bible says in I John 5:18, *"...but he who has been born of God keeps himself, and the wicked one does not touch him."* Also in Ephesians 4:27, Paul admonishes us not to give place to the devil. This is all to tell us that whatever authority Satan gains in the earth is directly dependent on whatever ground man yields to him. Unfortunately, many unsuspecting souls have relinquished substantial grounds to Satan by which he continues to assert some authority in the earth.

But how has Satan been able to pull off this deception for so long? It is by the fruits of 'the tree of the knowledge of good and evil' that he is able to succeed against us. Unsurprisingly, it is by the fruit of the same tree that he tricked Adam and Eve to relinquish their God-given authority to administrate the earth. Therefore, in order to stop the further yielding of grounds to Satan, and take back whatever grounds he has already taken, we have to understand the nature of this tree, which is the subject of the next two chapters.

CHAPTER 4

THE TREE OF THE KNOWLEDGE OF GOOD AND EVIL:
The Lie of Instant Dominion

M ost Christians take for granted that the blessing of God for man to have dominion in the earth, as declared in Genesis Chapter One, is available only to believers. However, God's declaration, *"Let them have dominion..."* (Genesis 1:26), was made to Adam and Eve as representatives of all mankind. Thus, dominion in the earth is available to all men, both believers and unbelievers.

Also because Adam was created in the image and likeness of God, all men do possess attributes unique to the personhood of God. These God-attributes, by extension, qualify man to have dominion in the earth. Moreover, by making the tree of the knowledge of good and evil available to Adam and Eve, and commanding them not to eat of it, God demonstrated that He created man to be a free moral being with the capacity and privilege to choose his own destiny.

Having been created to *look* like God, and enabled to *act* like Him, man now has the capacity to do virtually everything for himself on this earth without God. Consequently, there is a real temptation for man to think he does not need God, and to begin to trust in his own strength and wisdom.

The rich is especially vulnerable to this temptation, because wealth reinforces this feeling of false self-sufficiency. This is the reason Jesus said that it would be difficult for the rich to enter into the kingdom of God. Jesus interpreted this statement to mean that those who trust in their riches would find it hard to enter God's kingdom (see Mark 10:24).

But only in regard to the natural world is unsaved man superior in anything. Unsaved man has zero authority in the spirit, being spiritually dead without Christ. Therefore, all unbelievers are also excluded from the vast spiritual wealth that is available to only those who have experienced a spiritual rebirth in Christ.

However, since man was created to function as a spirit being as well, his spiritual death implies a large spiritual void in his life. This void is what Satan exploits to offer a counterfeit spiritual experience and a feeling of well-being to the unsaved man.

A truly prosperous person, therefore, is wealthy both in the spirit realm and in the natural realm. And since all spiritual riches are fully vested in Christ alone, no one without a full relationship with Him can have full access to spiritual riches. A full relationship with Christ demands a complete union with Him, which necessitates total dependence on Him. Hence, Jesus' statement in John 15:5:

> I am the vine, you *are* the branches. He who abides in
> Me, and I in him, bears much fruit; **for without Me**
> **you can do nothing** (emphasis added).

The above foundation helps us to answer two difficult questions that have baffled the minds of God's people throughout the ages. First, how has man been able to accomplish so much in the world without God? Second, why do the unrighteous prosper while the saints of God are many times beset with problems? The latter question perplexed Job, and offended David (see Job 21:7 and Psalm78:16). Even today, these questions remain a dilemma and a source of both frustration and temptation for many Christians.

When believers are struggling in life, and unbelievers appear to be succeeding in their endeavors, the temptation is for believers to marginalize their own superior heritage, and to begin to covet what the world has. But believers must understand that the prosperity of the world is only temporarily and, in the end, a meaningless futility, as the Book of Ecclesiastics vividly portrays. Else, believers will continue to be victims of the deceitfulness of riches of this world, and will continue to neglect the true riches God has made available for them through Christ.

The goal of this chapter, therefore, is to present an understanding of 'the tree of the knowledge of good and evil' to explain why unbelievers can be successful in this present world, and why true believers could do so much better than everybody else on earth.

Let us begin by noting that God blessed Adam and Eve with full prosperity that affected every area of their lives. Remember, God's ultimate goal was for them to have dominion in the earth. To help Adam and Eve reach this goal, God empowered them to prosper saying,

> "...Be fruitful and multiply; fill the earth and subdue it; have dominion over the fish of the sea, over the birds of the air, and over every living thing that moves on the earth" (Genesis 1:28)

Because Adam and Eve failed, we are left wondering what exactly this blessing of dominion would look like if they had not failed.

We learned earlier that God gave man the right to choose his own destiny. This right implied that man could also choose how he would achieve dominion in the earth.

He could achieve dominion by totally submitting himself to the will of God or he could do so through his own effort and his own standard of what is right and wrong. Jesus also faced a similar choice during his ministry on earth: to achieve dominion by submitting to the will of God, or to do so by choosing Satan's offer of instant success.

We all know Adam's choice and the consequences that followed. Jesus, on the other hand, chose to submit himself to the will of God. Therefore, according to Philippians 2:5-11, God also exalted Jesus and gave him a name that is above every name that, at the mention of the name of Jesus, every knee would bow. That is full dominion!

Jesus' exaltation shows that, the supremacy Adam and Eve desired was to be found in submitting themselves to God, and not in seeking their own way. They wanted dominion, but they sought an alternative way of reaching dominion that would bypass God's government and authority.

This is the dilemma man without God has been trying to resolve throughout the ages: how to be totally free without the authority of God. But the farther man tries to move away from the authority of God, the more chaotic his world becomes, and the less true freedom he experiences. It was the fall of Adam and Eve that birthed this tendency in the heart of man.

The question is, what was so attractive about Satan's deception, which so easily provoked Adam and Eve to disobey God, disregarding the consequence? To get some answers, let us scrutinize Satan's offer to them. We will see that Satan offered Adam and Eve what appeared to be the path to *instant* dominion without God's authority. Mark the words of the deceiver:

> Then the serpent said to the woman, "You will not
> surely die. For God knows that in the day you eat of
> it your eyes will be opened and you will be like God,
> knowing good and evil" (Genesis 3:4-5).

The Hebrew word translated *'day'* in verse 5 is *'yom'*, and is from a root word that means *'to be hot'*. Satan was playing a mind game with Adam and Eve. We may paraphrase *'in the day'* to read, 'in the very heat of the day', or 'by the time the sun goes down'.

Satan was subliminally implanting in their minds that the transformation to becoming like God would be *instant*, as soon as they ate the fruit. If this supposition was true, then the puzzling question becomes, why would the opportunity to *instantly* become like God present a real source of temptation to Adam and Eve? After all, Genesis 1:26 shows that God intended to create man *according to His likeness.*

The answer is, they would not be tempted unless they were not already like God at this time. To see why this was the case, we have to know how God sees things in order to understand what He says about things. God lives outside of time and sees things in their completed end. The Bible says He calls things that are not yet in existence as though they were (see Romans 4:17). But it takes earthly time and process for us, as men, to see the manifestation of the completed end of what God does.

The point is, God created man with the *potential* to be like him. But it would take the *process of time* for man to fully experience God's divine nature, as we would learn later.

The Critical Omission

Let us examine Genesis chapter 1:26 and 27 a little closer to observe the accuracy of this assertion. In verse 26, God said, *"Let Us make man in Our image, **according to Our likeness...**"* But, note the conspicuous omission in verse 27: *"So God created man in His own image; in the image of God He created him..."* We are expecting a phrase similar to, *'**according to His likeness'** to complete the statement, to match v. 26, but it is missing in v. 27. Why this significant omission? The answer to this question is the reason Satan's offer to Adam and Eve was so tempting.

Two different Hebrew words are translated *image* and *likeness*. The original word translated *image* carries the meaning of a mere resemblance in appearance only. On the other hand, the word translated *likeness* implies a resemblance in manner (conduct, method) or similitude (equality, equivalence).

Do you see the picture? Adam had a glory about him that made him *look* like God. However, he only had the *potential* to act like God, a position he was destined to attain according to God's plan, as revealed in Genesis 1:26. Let me say it in plain English: Adam was dressed to look like God, but for him to think and act like God was going to take a process of time. *Image* could be bestowed instantly, but *likeness* had to be attained through a process in time!

Here is an example of this concept in the Book of John. Although all believers become the sons of God as soon as they are born again, the Bible is clear in John 1:12 that we are only given *the power to become* the sons of God when we believe in Christ. (Sons of God should be interpreted as a position or a title for all believers, regardless of gender.) So even though 1 John 3:2 says, *"Beloved, now are we the sons of God..."* Romans 8:19 says the whole of creation is *waiting* for the manifestation of the sons of God.

In other words, we are the sons of God in position or status, but not completely so in our experience. According to Ephesians 4:11-13, Christ gave to the Church the five-fold ministry gifts—apostles, prophets, evangelists, pastors, and teachers—to bring believers to experience the fullness of this 'Sonship' capacity.

Decoding the Tree of Knowledge

Now, let us attempt to decode the symbolism used in the story surrounding the tree of the knowledge of good and evil, which is the key to understanding the inherent power of the soul of man. Our brief study of the Hebrew text used in Genesis 1:26-27, presented earlier, led us to know that 'to be like God' implied to be *equal* or *equivalent* to God.

However, because God is the creator of everything, He is the ultimate authority to determine what is good and evil in the universe. The standards of good and evil are embodied in the commandments, laws, ordinances, and precepts that proceed from God. Whatever God allows is good; whatever He disallows is evil. Hence, eating the fruit of the tree of the knowledge of good and evil amounts to rejecting the authority of God.

So what? Well, Adam knew that he was expected to subdue the earth, and that it would take time to fully accomplish his mission. He would have to wait for God to take him step by step into dominion. And we are going to see how God does this in a moment. God's way was fine with Adam and Eve until the serpent showed up with a very tantalizing proposition:

"What if you could get all this dominion today, and all you have to do is eat the fruit of the tree that God does not want you to eat", the serpent hissed.

"But we will die if we eat or even touch it", Eve replied.

"Of course you will not die!" countered the serpent. *"God knows you will be instantly transformed to be like Him, and you would no longer need Him for anything. Imagine the ability to*

create everything your heart desires instantly instead of waiting for all eternity."

Adam's interest was aroused as he drew closer to the unfolding conversation. *"How does eating of this tree help you transform to look like God?"*

"Sir, you are missing the point", the serpent taunted Adam. *"This tree does not transform your image. You are already made in the image of God. What you lack is His knowledge and how He sees and does things." "This is why this tree is the best kept secret in the universe." "And now, you can see why God does not want you or anyone else to eat its fruits. Because, once you know what God knows, you will be free from Him forever."*

Adam wondered why the serpent was not as powerful as God, if he knew all these secrets; but the prospect of instantly becoming like God was too overpowering to risk losing the opportunity. He looked at Eve approvingly, as she plucked the forbidden fruit and shared it with him.

Okay, I am getting a little carried away by my imagination, but do you get the point? Adam knew he had been created with the potential to be like God, but he did not yet possess the experience of being like God. And here, in Satan's offer, was an instant way to achieve that goal without going through God's process.

When Adam and Eve ate the fruit of the forbidden tree, however, they did not attain dominion instantly. Instead, they felt they had lost something—their covering—and were filled with fear. They sewed fig leaves to cover themselves, even though what they needed was the more durable covering made out of animal's skins, such as the ones God made for them.

That was their first hint that the serpent had deceived them. The knowledge they had gained at the expense of disobeying God was incomplete! They had only enough knowledge to provide themselves with temporary comfort.

It is obvious Adam and Eve did not possess the likeness of God prior to their fall, and that God intended for them to grow into His likeness through a different process. This fact is evident in Genesis 3:22. After they ate the forbidden fruit, God said, *"Behold, the man **has become** like one of us, to know good and evil."* If Adam and Eve at the time before their fall already possessed the likeness of God, this statement would be somewhat meaningless.

Let us attempt to interpret the statement *"...the man has become like one of us to know good and evil."* God was not implying that Adam now possessed the full capacity of God. It was only in respect to knowing good and evil that they had become like God.

In other words, since God was the sole authority in the universe to set standards of good and evil, Adam's rejection of that authority meant that he had now become a god unto himself to set his own standards. In that limited sense, he had become like God.

I wish everyone could see the obvious lessons in all of this. Clearly, Satan's tactic has not changed over time. The thrill of instant gratification is still the pursuit of a world steeped in knowledge, but lacking contentment. This is the same thrill Satan offered Jesus in the temptation in the wilderness. If only Jesus would worship him, He (Jesus) could have instant access to the dominion Adam lost to Satan.

As we will learn later, complete dominion is possible only through the knowledge of God. Any knowledge void of God's revelation is incomplete knowledge. So let me reemphasize the point: the pathway to total dominion for man is total dependence on God. And total dependence on God equates to total obedience to Him.

I know the concept of dominion conditioned upon total obedience appears illogical to some at this time, and I will resolve the apparent paradox later. However, it is crucial that we understand this principle of total dependence on God; else the whole notion of the kingdom of God, and the experience of its incredible power will continue to elude us, as Christians. In fact, as we will also learn later in this chapter, the New Covenant, which is the foundation for life in Christ, is based solely on this principle of total dependence on God.

Yet because man can do so much for himself already without God, it is hard for him to understand his need for total dependence on God. The soul of man inherited substantial powers from Adam by which man can often seem self-sufficient. This was Adam's choice. He chose the path of self-determination, where he would explore and determine his own standards of right and wrong. Nevertheless, being dead in his spirit implied that Adam could conquer and rule the earth only by his knowledge of observable facts in the natural world. Herein is the basis of science, as we know it.

Unsurprisingly, today, man's efforts have taken him to the uttermost frontiers of scientific knowledge. Without God, he has achieved fantastic breakthroughs in all facets of life on earth. Yet his world is still overwhelmed by problems for which he seems to find no answers.

Let me clarify, however, that the pursuit of science is not necessarily against God's will. On the contrary, God's assignment for man to subdue the earth implied the application of science. We learn in Proverbs 2:25 that *"it is the glory of God to conceal a thing: but the honor of kings is to search out a matter"*, and searching out a matter that God has concealed in the universe is what all sciences are about. The problem with Adam's choice, therefore, was not about the acquisition of knowledge but rather the source of his knowledge.

God's plan was for Adam and Eve to discover their full potential through their knowledge of God. And, as they discovered God, they would also be empowered to exercise dominion in the earth. Since Adam and Eve were created in God's image, and endowed with God's attributes, they would begin to know their own abilities and potential, as they became acquainted with the person of God. This was, and still is, the basic premise of God's plan of dominion for man.

Everything Adam and Eve needed to have dominion in the earth was in God. But nothing that they needed was automatically available to them. They had to exercise their choice, and acknowledge God as their source to obtain anything in God. This was the reason for the existence of the tree of the knowledge of good and evil in the Garden of Eden. It forever signified to them their complete freedom to choose God's way or follow their own path.

If they would choose God's way, they would discover their creative abilities through impartation and revelation by the Holy Spirit. That meant Adam and Eve could know things directly without experimentation. God knows all things without study or experience because, *"Nothing in all creation can hide from him. Everything is naked and exposed before his eye" (Hebrews 4:13 – NLT)*.

How much misery could have been avoided on earth, if man knew the right idea the first time; and how much more pain could have been prevented, if he knew the right idea only for the right purpose. But science without God has often led to dangerous experimentations and unintended awful consequences.

It was through the process of knowing God that man would have realized his ultimate destiny of being like God, and having all things under his feet as revealed in Psalm 8. Knowing God was going to be a perpetual process whereby man would continually be transformed into the *likeness* of God, as he came to know God more and more.

For it is impossible for man to ever grasp the fullness of an infinite God. God and His ways are past finding out. This is how Job 11:7, 8 puts it: *"Can you solve the mysteries of God? Can you discover everything there is to know about the Almighty? Such knowledge is higher than the Heavens."* It is in the context of man being continuously transformed into the image of God that Psalm 8 says that God created man a little lower than *Himself* (*Elohim* in Hebrew—see v. 5). The Truth is, for all eternity, man is going to continually discover, and be awed by the incredible glory of God.

But as we have come to understand, Adam had the freedom to choose an alternative path to dominion. He could also discover his world and his potential through the fruits of the 'Tree of the Knowledge of Good and Evil'. And, sadly, that is the alternative they chose.

Apart from representing the capacity to exercise moral choices without God's authority, the 'Tree of the Knowledge of Good and Evil' also represented the acquisition of knowledge without God's revelation. This translates into: the philosophical and scientific inquiry into nature, and the discovery of knowledge as to the 'what and how' of life without God's revelation. Most religions, including 'New Age', have their roots in this way of self-discovery.

The Bible says that:

> For since the creation of the world God's *invisible qualities*—his eternal power and divine nature—have been clearly seen, *being understood from what has been made*, so that men are without excuse (Romans 1:20—NIV).

The above Scripture shows that man could gain some knowledge about God and himself by studying creation. For instance, by studying different animals we are able to know how our own body functions. This is where evolutionists went wrong.

The similarities between man and animals are not evidence of evolution, but of the stamp of ownership by God in everything He created. Note that the similarities end only in regard to the natural body, because both were made out of the same material—dirt. Man is further differentiated from all animals by an additional attribute, which is his spirit.

The problem with knowledge that is the result of studying nature is that it is limited to a three-dimensional view. This is the problem of science as we know it. It is limited to what we can see, feel, hear, smell and touch. But there is a fourth dimension—the spiritual dimension—that deals with what *"No eye has seen, no ear has heard, and no mind has imagined what God has prepared for those who love him"* (1 Corinthians 2:9—NLT).

Yes, what man can discover about God in nature is what God has chosen to reveal about Himself. However, there are invisible things of God that can only be apprehended in the spirit. First Corinthians 2:11 and 14 show that man in his natural state cannot receive spiritual things, and that only the Holy Ghost can know the things of God. In order for man to know God, therefore, he has to be born again of the Spirit. Thereafter, the Holy Spirit can begin to impart the knowledge of God to him.

John 4:24 throws an interesting light on God's perspective on man's nature. The Scripture reads: *God is Spirit, and those who worship Him must worship in spirit and truth."* If God demands that we relate to Him only at the spirit level, as John 4:24 is implying, then, becoming like God, which is the prerequisite for achieving dominion in the earth, is a spiritual transformation.

This transformation is effected through the knowledge of God, as we briefly saw earlier. To put it bluntly, we cannot achieve dominion in the earth without knowing God. Therefore, no matter how great man becomes at science, he will never achieve complete dominion in the earth without the revelation of who God is.

The above discussion makes it is easier for us to understand why unbelievers can be successful in this world, even if their achievements are limited or temporary. Some are able to achieve significant success through the fruits of the knowledge of good and evil.

These are people who have become gods unto themselves and make up their own moral standards, as they go through life. To these folks, there are no absolute truths in the world. Truth then becomes whatever feels good in the sight of a person at any particular time.

Other people are also able to achieve a measure of success by bowing down to Satan, who empowers them with false success. These are people who have sold their souls to Satan (through Satan's deception or by their own choice) to manifest all kinds of evil in the earth. Nevertheless, whatever success man without God attains under the sun, he is still subject to the futility and meaninglessness of life that the Book of Ecclesiastics so eloquently describes.

CHAPTER 5

DOMINION THROUGH THE KNOWLEDGE OF GOD: God's Only Way!

L et us consider again the fact that it is through the knowledge of God that we become like God. And by being like God, we are able to exercise full dominion in the earth.

God's original plan as to how man would attain dominion in the earth has not changed. Throughout the Scriptures, God makes it plain His number one purpose for relating to man through covenants is for man to know Him. In the New Covenant, God expresses this thought as: *"I will be their God, and they will be my people."*

The heart-cry of the Apostle Paul in Philippians 3:10-14 was:

> **That I may know Him** and the power of His resur-
> rection, and the fellowship of His sufferings, being
> conformed to His death, if, by any means, I may
> attain to the resurrection from the dead. Not that I
> have already attained, or am already perfected; but I
> press on, that I may lay hold of that for which Christ
> Jesus has also laid hold of me. Brethren, I do not
> count myself to have apprehended; but one thing

I do, forgetting those things which are behind and reaching forward to those things which are ahead, I press toward the goal for *the prize of the upward call of God in Christ Jesus.*

"The prize of the upward call of God in Christ Jesus" that Paul talks about is not just a greater ministry than he had at the time. The high calling of God for all His people is to be conformed to the image of Christ; to experience His divine nature; to be molded into His likeness—This is the 'upward' calling of God to all mankind!

Paul knew that whatever level of the knowledge of God and of Christ he had attained, there was yet much more to be apprehended. Therefore, in order to apprehend deeper truths in God, he could not afford to rest on his past successes.

The Scripture is very clear that it is through the knowledge of God that we are transformed into the likeness of God or share in His divine nature. This is the thought expressed in 2 Peter 1:2-4:

Grace and peace be yours in abundance *through the knowledge of God* and of Jesus our Lord. His divine power has given us everything we need for life and godliness *through our knowledge of him* who called us by his own glory and goodness. Through these he has given us his very great and precious promises, so that through them **you may participate in the divine nature** and escape the corruption in the world caused by evil desires (NIV—emphasis added).

The more intimately we know God, the more we will trust Him, and the more we will believe His promises by which we share in the divine nature of God, as we just read above. Everything we will ever need or desire is in God. He wants man to know that He is the only God, and that He is all man needs. Therefore, it is in the best interest of man to know all he can about God. The following Scriptures speak to God's priority for man:

> "But you are my witnesses, O Israel!" says the LORD. "And you are my servant. *You have been chosen to know me*, believe in me, and understand that I alone am God" (Isaiah 43:10—NLT).

> My people are being destroyed because they don't *know me*. (Hosea 4:6— NLT)

> *Knowledge of the Holy* One results in understanding. (Proverbs 9:10—NLT)

> For I desire mercy and not sacrifice, and the *knowledge of God* more than burnt offerings (Hosea 6:6).

God's primary objective has always been to have a living relationship with man based on love alone—a love relationship where man comes to know God enough to trust Him with all. (In Chapter 10, we will understand that God's objective in getting man to love Him and to trust Him is for the benefit of man and not for God.)

Therefore, the code of laws that was given to Israel was not God's preferred way of establishing a relationship with Israel. As Paul argues throughout his epistles to the Galatians and Romans, the purpose of the Law was never to secure salvation for man. Rather, it was to demonstrate how guilty man was, and how impossible it was for man to gain salvation through his own efforts. So we now begin to understand why the old covenant was regarded as inadequate to address both man's problem and God's objective, and why God had to enact a new covenant in place of the old.

The New Covenant

Let us take a look at the new covenant and see how radically different it is from the Law given through Moses.

> "The time is coming," declares the LORD, "when I will make a new covenant with the house of Israel and with the house of Judah. It will not be like the covenant I made with their forefathers when I took

them by the hand to lead them out of Egypt, because
they broke my covenant, though I was a husband to
them," declares the LORD. "This is the covenant I
will make with the house of Israel after that time,"
declares the LORD. "I will put my law in their minds
and write it on their hearts. I will be their God, and
they will be my people. No longer will a man teach
his neighbor, or a man his brother, saying, 'Know
the LORD,' because they will all know me, from the
least of them to the greatest," declares the LORD...
(Jeremiah 31:31-34).

Here in the New Covenant, God is reflecting on the inadequacy
of the Law of Moses as the basis of relating to Israel. Under the Old
Covenant, man's relationship with God was based on externalities
that were incapable of changing the heart of man. They were a set
of codes that had to be memorized and obeyed to affect the heart.
Under the New Covenant, man's relationship with God originates
from a heart that has been fashioned to know and obey God—the
heart motivating the outward actions of man.

The question that is easy to overlook in the New Covenant is
how was God so sure that, this time, man would not break His law
as the people did under the Old Covenant? God speaks emphatically
in verses 33 and 34 of Jeremiah 31: *"I will be their God, and they
will be My people."* And also, *"...they will all know Me, from the
least of them to the greatest..."* How is God going to accomplish this
with certainty? If this *new thing* still depended on man's ability and
faithfulness, then we cannot be so sure. Well, God has an answer
that is good news for man. Listen to how God does it:

> *I will give you a new heart and put a new spirit within
> you*; I will take the heart of stone out of your flesh
> and give you a heart of flesh. *I will put My Spirit
> within you and cause you to walk in My statutes*, and
> you will keep My judgments and do them. Then you
> shall dwell in the land that I gave to your fathers; *you*

> *shall be My people, and I will be your God.* (Ezekiel
> 36:26-28— emphasis added)

This passage in Ezekiel complements the promise of a new covenant in Jeremiah 31. In fact, they both have the same goal: that Israel would be God's people and that God will be their God. The passage in Ezekiel talks about how God would accomplish the goals of the New Covenant in Jeremiah 31.

Before God can write His law in the heart of the people, He will first take the old heart away and give them a new one. And before the people can know God, He will first give them a new spirit and then His own Spirit, who will teach them the knowledge of God. This is why, in Jeremiah 31, God states emphatically: *"No longer will a man teach his neighbor, or a man his brother, saying, 'Know the LORD..."*

Jesus also promised that, when the Holy Spirit come He would lead us into all truth (John 16:13). And listen to 1 John 2:27, which also echoes the fact that we would not need to be taught by anyone else, because the Holy Spirit Himself would be our teacher:

> But the anointing which you have received from
> Him abides in you, and you do not need that anyone
> teach you; but as the same anointing teaches you
> concerning all things, and is true, and is not a lie, and
> just as it has taught you, you will abide in Him.

The New Living Translation (NLT) interprets the Greek word that means *anointing* to be the Holy Ghost. This interpretation is in line with the passages quoted in Jeremiah and Ezekiel above. This is also confirmed in 1 Corinthians 2:12: *"Now we have received, not the spirit of the world, but the Spirit who is from God, **that we might know** the things that have been freely given to us by God."* Yes, the Holy Spirit will teach us and guide us into all truth. And the truth to which He leads us is not a bunch of abstract concepts, but a real person, even the Lord Jesus Christ (see John 16:11 and John 14:6).

Looking at the New Covenant, the most profound revelation about it was that there was no way for God's people to break it. It was fail-proof by design. Everything depended on God's power and faithfulness.

It was God who would give them a new heart; it was God who would put His Spirit within them; and it was God who would cause them to walk in His laws. Since nothing in this covenant depended on man, there was no place for them to fail. That is why God was so certain in Jeremiah 31 that Israel would *know* Him, because He would be their teacher, and He would be teaching them from a new heart that He was going to give them.

Today, we as Christians have been made partakers of the New Covenant through Christ, and we stand to gain from all its blessings. Through this New Covenant, God is saying to man again: the way to have complete dominion in the earth is through the knowledge of God. The way to have abundance of grace and peace is through the knowledge of God. The way to have all things that pertain to life and Godliness is through the knowledge of God. The way to procure God's divine nature is through His knowledge.

Isaiah 11 describes a world at peace under the government of Christ during His millennium reign. This Scripture shows a picture of an earth that is largely restored and the wickedness of men and the savagery of beast utterly subdued under the reign of Christ. This is the picture of full dominion in the earth, as God originally intended for Adam and Eve. And what would be responsible for this break-through in the earth?

> For the earth shall be full of **the knowledge of the Lord** (Isaiah 11:9b).

So the Scripture is unambiguous in showing that the heavenly condition that will exist during the millennium reign of Christ will be due to abundance of the knowledge of God in the earth.

It is evident from the above discussion that God does not want us to depend on our own understanding in anything, because the New Covenant, which is the basis for our union with Christ, has no provision for man's effort. The only responsibility for man is to believe and to yield to the workings of the Spirit of God in us. Jesus affirms this understanding in John 6:28:

> Then they said to Him, "What shall we *do*, that we may work the works of God?" Jesus answered and said to them, "This is the work of God, that you *believe* in Him whom He sent.

This Scripture reveals the stumbling block upon which all men fall in trying to reach God. Man is looking to *do* something to earn God's approval. God is looking for somebody who will just believe what He says.

Thus, faith is the *effort* man has to exercise to appropriate the blessing of the New Covenant. And faith is necessary because of God's irrevocable gift of choice to man—the freedom for man to choose his own destiny. In other words, man ought to be able to trust God enough to believe what He says, and to choose the way He points to him.

The requirement for faith in the things of God will never change. And that is why Jesus taught us to pray always and never give up (see Luke 18:1). Therefore, in Ezekiel 36, even after God promised He was going to restore Israel by His own ability and faithfulness, He adds in verse 37:

> This is what the Sovereign LORD says: "I am ready to hear Israel's prayers for these blessings, and I am ready to grant them their requests" (NLT).

The requirement for faith is also the reason why salvation is available to only those who *"call on the name of the Lord"* (Romans 10:13).

So if our dominion in the earth can only be achieved through our knowledge of God, then we can argue that much of the frustrations we encounter in life are, often, the results of walking by our own understanding instead of walking by the knowledge of God that the Holy Spirit teaches. Proverbs 16:25 warns us, *"There is a way that seems right to a man, but its end is the way of death."* And then in Hosea 6:4: *"My people are being destroyed because they don't know Me."*

When man does not know God, he makes life decisions based on the imperfect knowledge of past experiences and currently observable facts. The result of such decisions has been the attainment by man of stunning progress combined with equally stunning negative side effects, as we mentioned earlier.

Nevertheless, man continues to ignore God in his decision process with foolhardy stubbornness, being misled by explosion of intellectual knowledge and spectacular advances in technology. The promises held by scientific breakthroughs continue to fuel the lie that man can solve any problem given enough time.

Accordingly, there is an increased passion in the world today: a push to devote more and more resources for research, and a push to overthrow laws that restrain human excesses and abuses in medical research. We cannot begin to calculate the amount of money and other resources that the world has poured into research and development in recent years, all in the hope of getting solutions to current or imagined problems. And even though significant social, economic, and technological problems still abound, the belief remains that, with time, nothing would be impossible to man.

But here is the futility that will never go away: dominion in the earth is impossible without the knowledge of God; and coming into the knowledge of God is impossible without complete dependence on Him.

> As the Scriptures say, "I will destroy human wisdom and discard their most brilliant ideas." So where does this leave the philosophers, the scholars, and the world's brilliant debaters? God has made them all look foolish and has shown their wisdom to be useless nonsense. Since God in his wisdom saw to it that the world would never find him through human wisdom... (1Corinthians 1:19-21—NLT)

CHAPTER 6

THE TREE OF THE KNOWLEDGE OF GOOD AND EVIL:
Walking By Your Own Light

Now, let us take another look at *the tree of the knowledge of good and evil* which presents us with an interesting question: Why was the *good* of this tree forbidden together with the *evil* of the tree? In the answer to this question lays the trap for many people in the world. Herein is why many 'good-natured' people may end up in Hell and some seemingly undeserving people end up inheriting the earth, as the Bible teaches. It is because of the delusion about the self-righteousness of man that makes it important to revisit the subject of the 'tree of knowledge of good and evil'.

The reason the righteousness of man does not measure up to God's holiness is that God is not dealing with man on the basis of actions alone but the source of those actions as well—whether those actions are from the spirit or the flesh. The following true story, typical of so many well-meaning believers, best illustrates the point being made here.

The Danger of Evangelizing Without God's Light

Phillip (not his real name, of course), a vibrant Christian, had his eyes set on a lady (let us call her Joan) he had recently met. Upon learning that Joan was an unbeliever, he made it his passion to win Joan to Christ. Joan appeared to be receptive to the idea of being born again, and opened herself up barely enough to keep Phillip interested in her.

Phillip believed he had all but won Joan to Christ, so when Joan told him she was going to visit her family one weekend, he thought it would be a great idea to go and fortify her with some practical wisdom to deal with her unbelieving family. He had noticed that whenever Joan went away to visit her family, she always came back less enthusiastic about spiritual things.

He did not think of any other danger that would make his trip to Joan's apartment an unwise one at the time. Joan had a roommate, so Phillip made sure her roommate would be in the apartment during his visit. That fact alone emboldened him to set out to see Joan that evening.

But the Holy Spirit knew other things Phillip did not know. Phillip revealed later, "I had this tug in my gut and a ringing sound in my ear: *"Do not go to witness to Joan today."* For many of us, our immediate reaction to such a voice would be, "Get behind me, Satan!" And that was exactly how Phillip reacted. He started rebuking the voice in his spirit, and firmly resolved not to give in to the lie of the devil. So he pressed on *"like a lamb on his way to the slaughter"* (Proverbs 7:22, 23). Needless to say, that voice was the Holy Spirit warning him about a trap that had been set for his downfall.

When Phillip arrived at Joan's apartment, the first thing he noticed was that Joan was alone. Her roommate, he learned, had also decided to leave town that evening on a short notice. Dismissing the significance of that new development, he decided to press through and complete his mission for that evening.

To get to the main goal of his visit without appearing aggressive, he began with an unrelated subject. Before long, however, there were flirtatious exchanges; before long, there were romantic handholding; before long, there were passionate kisses. Before long…well, a bewildered Phillip woke up next to a half-naked Joan in bed.

And that was when his seven-year nightmare began! Not only had he compromised his testimony before Joan, he had also greatly bruised her fragile conscience from that time forward. For the next seven years, Phillip came to understand why the devil earned the title *"the accuser of our brethren"* (Revelation 12:10). As Phillip struggled desperately to regain his spiritual momentum, the devil spared no opportunity to harass him with the guilt of his indiscretion.

We all can see with hindsight how immature Phillip's actions were, and how a small dose of common sense could have prevented the unfortunate outcome to this story. Some of us may think that Phillip should have turned and run as soon as he noticed Joan was going to be alone with him that evening. Others may also think that Phillip should have scheduled the meeting outside of her apartment; or that he should have done the visitation together with another person.

However, these alternatives, prudent as they seem, were not the reasons Phillip failed. Each of those alternative decisions would have been good counsel, but they all fail to address the core of Phillip's problem. Phillip got what came to him because he leaned on his own understanding, and trusted in his own strength.

I have known men who, led by the Holy Spirit, were able to bring to Christ prostitutes so hardened in their bondage that no one thought they could be saved. I have also heard of great women of faith who performed similar feats in the lives of men hardened by all kinds of vices. In doing the will of God, these spiritual men and women took actions that, at first, appeared unwise. Nevertheless, because they were all under the guidance and protection of the Holy Spirit, they were able to achieve incredible success stories with the lives of those derelicts they helped.

Indeed, Phillip's failure was in trying to fulfill the will of God, trusting in his own strength and understanding. Had Phillip had an attitude of complete dependence on God, he would not have been too quick to dismiss the voice of the Holy Ghost, mistaking it for the voice of the devil. He should have known also that it is not the act of witnessing but obedience that pleases God.

The Bible is plain on this point in the story of King Saul: *"... Behold, to obey is better than sacrifice"* (I Samuel 15:22). Saul fell out of favor with God when he violated this principle. To Saul, the act of sacrificing to God became more important than obeying the voice of God.

Not that there was anything wrong with Saul's intention per se. On the contrary, God had always demanded sacrifices from his people, and an occasion of a victory in war was, arguably, the most appropriate time to offer a sacrifice of thanksgiving to God. But the point is, God specifically commanded a different action for that particular occasion. And that is all that matters in the kingdom of God. In kingdom life, the word of the King is supreme (see Ecclesiastics 8:4—RSV), and trumps all other decisions.

Here is another example from the story of Abraham. Abraham and Sarah got into trouble because they also relied on their own understanding regarding the promise of God.

God had told them that He would give them a child in their old age, even though they were past childbearing. However, when time appeared to erode any possibility of God's promise ever coming to pass, Sarah's logic machine went to work on behalf of God: "Maybe God did not necessarily mean the seed would come directly through me." So she reasoned that she could claim the child of her slave as her own child, because the owner of a slave owns everything the slave has. Therefore, giving her slave girl to Abraham to marry would help fulfill God's promise. "God certainly works in mysterious ways", she probably chuckled to herself in self-satisfaction.

Needless to say, that was the logic that produced Ishmael. Without seeking God first, Abraham and Sarah decided to fulfill God's will for their lives by their own wisdom.

We cannot fully comprehend what the consequences of that one act outside of God's will have had on human history. But, it was never peaceful in Abraham's house from the moment the seed of their self-will entered the planet earth.

In Acts 16:6-10, Paul and Silas wanted to go to Phrygia and Galatia to evangelize, but the bible says *"they were forbidden by the Holy Spirit to preach the word in Asia"*. Then, they tried to go to Bithynia and, again, *the Spirit did not permit them* (vs.6 and 7).

84

Later, however, the Holy Spirit directed them in a dream to go and preach the gospel to the people of Macedonia.

We can see the maturity and spiritual sensitivity of Paul and Silas clearly demonstrated in these Scriptures. They understood that the commission of Christ for them to go into all the world and preach the gospel did not relieve them of their daily dependence on God's provision and guidance. If they had pressed on to preach in any of those forbidden territories, they may have had great meetings, but they would not have accomplished anything of spiritual value.

We can save ourselves a lot of frustration in our walk with God, if we simply believe this revelation by Paul: *"For I know that in me (that is, in my flesh) nothing good dwells"* (Romans 7:18). At the risk of overemphasis, let say this again: there is nothing good that can come out of the flesh of man—the old Adamic nature. It is forever judged and condemned. It is completely dead in the eyes of God, and cannot be restored to any value in the spirit. *"So then, those who are in the flesh **cannot** please God"* (Romans 8:8).

This is why, in the new birth experience, God totally rejects everything belonging to our old nature, both good and bad. Hence, Paul can say in 2 Corinthians 5:17, *"Therefore, if anyone is in Christ, he is a new creation; old things have passed away; behold, all things have become new"*. Do you get the picture? We do not carry anything from our flesh (old nature) into Christ. Therefore, everything we do on this earth as believers should be done from the position of our *new man* in Christ.

Now, let us get back to Phillip's story. According to him, he was more embarrassed for looking like a hypocrite before Joan than compromising his walk in Christ. He did not have any doubt God would forgive him. But he was haunted by the thought of losing his credibility as a genuine witness before Joan, and with that, the possibility of losing her to the world again.

That latter thought plagued his conscience for a long time. Phillip says it took him more than seven years and a lot of assurances of God's love to forgive himself for what happened that fateful night. Today, Phillip is a wiser and a more effective witness for Christ, even though the scars from his past indiscretion are still visible in his present life.

Sadly, however, Phillip is one of the few fortunate ones who are able to recover lost spiritual grounds after trusting in themselves and giving in to the flesh. Others have not been so fortunate. Many powerful men of God have been brought to desolation as a result of leaning on their own strength and understanding in doing God's will. Some never recovered from their fall. Others have been crippled forever, and will never walk straight again.

The moral of Phillip's story bears emphasizing: In spiritual life, relying on human strength or wisdom is not only unprofitable, it is a devastating blunder. As we learned in the previous chapter, we can accomplish great things in this world without God.

Consequently, we face a real temptation to take God for granted or to ignore Him altogether. But if we truly want to make spiritual progress, then we must believe what Jesus told his disciples: *"... Without me, you can do nothing* (John 15:5). Jesus was not mincing any words—nothing that we do outside of him has any value in God's Kingdom.

Therefore, as believers desiring to do God's will, we must have an unwavering attitude of complete dependence on Him. We must trust only in the guidance of the Holy Spirit and in the strength supplied by Him. Hence, we must also be able to hear from God in order to walk in His will consistently. And when we hear God's word, that word overrides everything that conflicts with it, no matter how good or scriptural that thing may seem.

"...All our righteousnesses are like filthy rags" (Isaiah 64:6)

The fact that our natural goodness is unprofitable in spiritual life is difficult for many believers to receive. How can good be evil? Or, put in the context of Phillip's story, how can the voice of God seemingly contradict something as scriptural as going to witness to an unbeliever?

In order to solve this dilemma, we need to understand that when God speaks to us, He never contradicts His own Scriptures. Rather, the word God speaks to our spirit illuminates Scripture. Without this illumination from God, the mere letter of the Scriptures can kill, as Paul suggests in 2 Corinthians 3:6. Even hate-groups, such as the Ku

Klux Klan, quote the Scriptures to support their hatred; and so do many religious fanatics justify their actions of cruelty by the letter of the Scriptures.

What makes the Scriptures come alive is the breath of God—the Holy Spirit—upon the written word. And the Scriptures brought to life by God's Spirit cannot fail to produce life in those who hear and do them. Do not be fooled, Satan will use the letter of the Scriptures to deceive you, if you let him. That is why it is so critical to have an ear to hear from God.

We have to be able to hear from God because of the New Covenant by which we are brought into a relationship with the Father through the blood of Jesus. Under the New Covenant, there is no room for human strength or human wisdom as we learned in Chapter 5. The New Covenant predicates the believer's success entirely on God's faithfulness.

This was one of the main reasons God gave us His Spirit to dwell in us, so that the goal of the covenant will be realized, which is for us to know God and to become His people. Unless the Holy Spirit helps us, no stretch of human effort or wisdom can produce this goal in us.

In fact, the Greek word Jesus used to describe the Holy Spirit, *Paraclete*, implies that the Holy Spirit would be everything for us on behalf of Christ. Just imagine the dismay in the faces of the disciples, when Jesus told them he was leaving them to go to the Father. Only a few moments before, he had told the disciples they could do nothing without him. So when he turned around and announced that he was leaving them to go to the Father, they were stunned.

But Jesus deliberately produced this uneasiness in the disciples to focus them on one thing: that they would value the presence of the Holy Spirit with the same esteem they gave Jesus. He was trying to assure them that, through the Holy Spirit, he (Jesus) was going to be with them forever.

So the point is, if we have the Spirit of God dwelling in us, and He is everything to us, then we do not need anyone else to teach us to know God, as we saw in Chapter 5. Seeing then that God has gone to great lengths to teach us by His Spirit, we may also conclude that no amount of studying or intelligence can lead us to the truth, if God does not directly impart truth to us by His Spirit. Because, as Jesus asserted in John 14:17 and, again, in 16:13, it was the Holy Spirit that would lead us into *all* truth.

Does this mean that God does not use other people to teach us anything? No, for it is the same God who sets ministry gifts in the church to equip us with knowledge and understanding that will bring us to full maturity in Christ (see Ephesians 4:11-13). In fact, God teaches us using various media, and we will examine some of those during our discussion of spiritual hearing in the Chapter 8.

However, regardless of how God's word gets to us, it is the indwelling Holy Spirit, who will cause us to understand the will of God for us in the particular word we hear. It is this inner witness or inspired knowledge that no one can teach you except the Holy Spirit Himself. If we are not to lean on our own understanding, then we need to have this inner teaching of the Holy Spirit to know the will of God in everything.

In All Your Ways Acknowledge God!

If we believe the Holy Spirit dwells in us, then we have no excuse to walk in our own wisdom and strength at any time. And, even after we have come to know the will of God by His Spirit, our dependence on God does not end there. We must also fulfill God's will in God's time and in God's way.

Abraham and Sarah thought they were doing the will of God when they produced Ishmael. Jacob and Rebecca thought they were helping the will of God when they deceived Isaac for the blessing. Joshua thought he was fulfilling the will of God when he attacked the city of Ai without consulting God. The failures of these great people of God and others in the Bible teach us one thing: we need to acknowledge God in all we do to expect good success every time.

This is the revelation underlying the heart-cry of David in Psalm 27:4:

> One thing I have desired of the Lord, that I will seek:
> That I may dwell in the house of the Lord all the days
> of my life, to behold the beauty of the Lord and to
> inquire in His temple.

Notice, the phrase, *"all the days of my life"*, applies to dwelling in God's house, beholding the beauty of the Lord and inquiring in his temple. That means, David was seeking a place in his life where all his decisions would be based on the counsel of the Lord and not on his own understanding.

In the above Psalm, *"The temple of the Lord"* and *"the house of the Lord"* both represent our human spirits, where God dwells and communes with us. So what David by revelation was seeking after in Psalm 27:4 quoted above was to have all his decisions and actions arise from within his spirit and not from his soul realm (will, emotions and intellect). In the New Testament, this is equivalent to walking by the spirit, in contrast to walking by the flesh.

Proverbs 8:34, in speaking of wisdom (which we will later discover is the proceeding word of God), enunciates the same concept: *"Blessed is the man who listens to me, **watching daily** at my gates, waiting at the posts of my doors."* Yes, God wants us to seek His wisdom, provision and strength daily.

We have already seen how some great people of God failed because they neglected to seek God about some decisions they made. And we must also learn that seeking God daily was the secret behind the success of David, Daniel and all the other great people of God mentioned in the Bible. In 2 Chronicles 26:5, for instance, we are shown Uzziah's secret for being successful as a king over Israel: *"...and **as long as he sought the Lord**, God made him prosper."* Jesus was also unapologetic about his complete dependence on God for his success. In John 5:19 and 30, he asserted that he never did or said anything except as he saw or heard the Father do or say.

Make No Allowance for The Flesh!

We need to emphasize that there is no room for human wisdom or strength in the kingdom of God. God has already done all the work. Hebrews 4:3 declares that all of God's work was finished from the foundation of the world. This implies God has already determined the end from the beginning, and He holds the blueprint for getting to that future end. Our prayer should always remain *"Let your will be done on earth as it is in Heaven."*

All of our actions should, therefore, be in line with God's blue-print in heaven. He told Moses in Exodus 25:37 regarding the building of the Ark of the Covenant: *"Be sure that you make everything according to the pattern I have shown you here on the mountain."* God has a pattern for everything in His kingdom. But any time we mix God's pattern with our human wisdom, the blessing that results is also mixed.

We cannot overemphasize this truth: Nothing coming out of the flesh of man can ever accomplish God's will. That is why God regards our righteous acts that do not flow from our obedience to His will as filthy rags.

God is not moved at all even if we have great intentions in our self-righteous acts, because God acts solely from principles and not from emotions. His emotions are based on His principles and not vice versa. His mercy, grace, judgments and miracles are never haphazard, but are based on principles. And those principles He calls His 'word', 'law', 'statutes' or 'commands'. This is why He has magnified His word above all His name (Psalm 138:2).

John 1:1-3 is very definite about the indispensability of the word of God. It says, God did not create anything without Christ, who personifies the word of God. Since God birthed everything in the universe by His word, any activity of man that does not have its root in the word of God has no spiritual value in God's economy, regardless of that activity's virtue or apparent impact.

For the above reason, God will judge every work of man by fire (see 1 Corinthians 3:13-15). Nothing that originated in the flesh will survive the test by fire. And we repeat without reservation that God has already judged the flesh. It was crucified in Christ and can never be redeemed. Therefore, anything coming out of that nature is counted dead in the eyes of God.

Good intentions are commendable, but God looks solely at His word. This explains in part why God killed Uzzah when he touched the Ark of the Covenant on its way back to Israel (see 2 Samuel 6:6). Uzzah's action violated a law of God: that only the priests could touch the Ark. An uninformed person sees God as being too harsh in this episode. "After all, this man had good intentions," someone may argue.

But listen to Hebrews 1:3: all things are being upheld by the *word* of God's power. We cannot imagine what would happen if God acted purely out of emotions, and decided to ignore His own word in order to please man. This I know with certainty: God will never violate His own word. He will not alter the word that has gone out of His lips (Psalm 89:34). Jesus also said, *"...Till Heaven and earth pass away, one jot or one tittle will by no means pass from the law till all is fulfilled" (Matthew 5:18).*

Walking in The Light of Your Own Fire

What does all this mean? It is imperative we understand the pre-eminence of the word of God in all things, if we are going to enjoy the rich inheritance God has reserved for us in Christ Jesus. When we put our trust in human wisdom, the results are often dashed hopes and unmet expectations, both of which lead to unnecessary torment in our soul. In fact, we will do well to heed this rather severe warning from God in Isaiah 50:10-11:

> ...All you who light fires and provide yourselves with flaming torches, go, walk in the light of your fires and of the torches you have set ablaze. This is what you shall receive from my hand: You will lie down in torment.

Walking *in the light of your fires* is what Proverbs 3:5 calls *leaning on your own understanding.* We need fire for light, warmth and for sustenance (processing food). Lighting our own fires means making life decisions without God's direction. It also means seeking to fulfill our needs and desires without God's provisions.

But Jesus said we should pray to God to *"Give us this day our DAILY bread" (Matthew 6:11).* We are instructed to seek God daily and to seek His provisions for each day. This implies that our dependence on God is daily and not just for some of the time.

The principle of daily dependence on God was depicted in the instructions to the Israelites, concerning the gathering of manna in the wilderness. They were to take only what they would eat in a day. Anything more than a day's worth that was left overnight was infested with maggots (see Exodus 16:19-20). By implication, God was demanding that His people learn to trust Him daily for their sustenance.

But was God teaching us only about the provision of food for our daily sustenance? No. But more so, He was teaching us to seek Him for wisdom and direction for our lives daily. Hence, Proverbs 3:6: *"In all your ways acknowledge him and he will direct your path."* How many of your ways? Answer: ALL! Not only in the major decisions facing you, but also in the seemingly easy ones. This is why Jesus encouraged us to pray always and not to faint (Luke 18:1).

The reason God wants us to trust him in even the smallest of issues of life is that what we see as a small issue may be just the tip of the proverbial iceberg. What we call a *small* decision may have far reaching consequences in the future.

As we saw previously, Joshua discovered this truth in a very painful way. He was defeated by the city of Ai, the smallest of the cities he was to conquer, in spite of God's ironclad promise that no one would be able to stand against him all the days of his life (see Joshua 1:5 and 7:2-5). However, the condition for having good success in his life was careful obedience to the word of God (see Joshua 1:8).

In the battle for Jericho, Joshua consulted God, and God gave him a word of assurance and a strategy by which he won a great victory. However, in the battle against the city of Ai, Joshua reasoned that the city was so small he could capture it with only a small regiment of his army. Well, he was wrong. Someone had broken God's condition for victory, and Joshua did not know about it. But if Joshua had first consulted God, God would have revealed the problem to him. As it turned out, that small city was the only one on record that defeated Joshua in a battle.

"In all your ways acknowledge him and he will direct your path" is the foundation for all decisions and actions of a believer. As we alluded to earlier, a lot of tormenting issues facing many believers today can be traced to little decisions made without God's direction or provision.

God certainly wants us to make plans; that is why he instructs us in Proverbs 16:3: *"Commit your work to the LORD, and then your plans will succeed" (NLT)*. The problem is not with the making of decisions or plans, but rather with the source of those plans and the paths to achieving them. God wants us to initiate all actions from our regenerated spirit, who alone can hear from God, and know His will. To the extent that our plans or decisions are initiated from the soul (our intellect, will and emotions), we are still living by the fruits of "the tree of the knowledge of good and evil."

Certainly, because God created us natural beings on purpose, our natural endowments have a role to play in God's economy. We are not, therefore, minimizing the role of our intellect or our will in decision-making, for instance. Instead, we caution against assigning our natural faculties the wrong priorities in our lives.

We will show in Chapter 8 the appropriate roles for these natural faculties as God intended them to be used. For now, let us be mindful of what Galatians 5:17 says: that both the flesh and the Spirit are vying for preeminence in our life. Therefore, we should be careful not to hand the reins of our life to the flesh at any time.

Is it not surprising that we are so quick to profess the power of God and to shout about His promises; yet seeking God is not a high priority in our lives? Instead, we make God our last resort—when everything else fails.

The result of this tendency is that we have become an anemic body of believers with very little victory in our lives. We are constantly reminiscing on the good old days, and dreaming about a sweet 'by-and-by', when most of God's promises are available for our enjoyment now in this present life.

Many of us are plagued by the same curses, and are entangled in the same confusion that the world suffers. No wonder a large portion of the world is still not convinced that Jesus truly is the answer to the world's problems! No wonder unbelievers shun and mock the Church the way they do!

Why Believers Do Not Seek God Enough

I believe there are several reasons believers do not seek God as they should; and all of them trace back to the flesh. Due to the fall of Adam, there is a propensity in our old nature to rebel against the will of God. Thus, the flesh does not want to submit to God, and rejects the light of God. We have already learned that this propensity of the flesh cannot be cured. In fact, Romans 8 says the flesh *cannot* submit to the law of God. It seeks independence from all authority, so it can determine its own pleasure.

Therefore, when we walk by the flesh, there is an innate distrust of God at work in our heart, whether we are aware of it or not. We do not seek God always for fear He may not answer our prayers the way we desire or in the time we want.

We sometimes see our need as so urgent, and God's way too long that we are tempted to take matters into our own hands. That is the very nature of the flesh. The flesh loves pleasure, and cannot wait for a due season. Remember Satan's bait of *instant gratification* for Adam and Eve in Genesis chapter three?

There are times, however, when some believers genuinely think they know exactly what they need and how to get it. This is the temptation of putting logic and human strength before God's word. In doing so, however, these believers run afoul of the warning in Proverbs 14:12: *"There is a way that seems right to a man, but its end is the way of death"*.

But listen to God's heart in the following Scriptures and see if our fear or self-dependence is warranted:

- "For I know the plans I have for you," declares the LORD, "plans to prosper you and not to harm you, plans to give you hope and a future"(Jeremiah 29:11-NIV).
- "He who did not spare His own Son, but delivered Him up for us all, how shall He not with Him also freely give us all things"(Romans 8:32)?
- "If you then, being evil, know how to give good gifts to your children, how much more will your Father who is in Heaven give good things to those who ask Him" (Matthew 7:11)!
- "You open your hand and satisfy the desires of every living thing" (Psalm 145:16-NIV).
- "The Lord is not slow in keeping his promise, as some understand slowness" (2Peter 3:9-NIV).
- "The blessing of the Lord makes one rich, and He adds no sorrow with it" (Proverbs 10:22).

- "I have come that they may have life, and that they may have *it* more abundantly" (John 10:10).

Every believer ought to have an abundant life, because God has provided for our every need and desire. The Bible says that every good gift and every perfect gift comes from God. He is the Father of lights and there is no shadow or variableness in Him (James 1:17). God is the source of pure joy. His kingdom is *"righteousness, peace and joy in the Holy Ghost"* (Romans 14:17). He delights in the prosperity of his people. He loves to see us victorious, and is thrilled to see us celebrate our victories.

Everything about God is positive. This is how the Psalmist describes the atmosphere surrounding God: *"In Your presence is fullness of joy; At Your right hand are pleasures forevermore"* (Psalm 16:11). Joy and pleasures for evermore! Does this sound like a God who is too serious to have any fun at all?

The problem is we do not see God in this agreeable light, because the enemy has deceived us as to what is true joy and pleasure. We are so used to gratifying the carnal cravings of our flesh that we limit pleasure and joy only to our base nature.

Some years ago, God, through his infinite grace, gave me a glimpse of this "joy in the Holy Ghost." First Peter 1:8 describes this joy as *"unspeakable and full of glory"*, and I can now appreciate why. All I can say about the experience I had is that there is nothing in this world at the present time that can give such joy. I do not believe we have the appropriate vocabulary in this life to describe that level of ecstasy. I do not even believe our natural body in its current state can contain the fullness of that joy I was privileged to experience.

Here is the point: God wants to bring us to that perfect joy, peace, and love that define his kingdom. Yet we continually wonder if God means what He says, and not being sure He does, we take comfort in our own strength. But listen again to Jesus: *"If you then, being evil, know how to give good gifts to your children, how much more will your Father who is in Heaven give good things to those who ask Him"* (Matthew 7:11)!

Perhaps the biggest reason we struggle to see God in this all-loving disposition is that, when God revealed Himself and His righteousness in the dispensation of the Law, under the Old Covenant, He was dealing with the stubbornness of man's heart. He was teaching man the utter futility of trying to earn salvation through self-effort. And in doing so, He was also preparing man for the New Covenant that was to be put into effect through the blood of Jesus.

But the severity of God towards the Jews in the wilderness also demonstrated His heartache towards man. Man is consistently turning away from God to seek pleasures in all the wrong places and things, when all he needs is in God Himself. God is saying through His austerity that everything in the universe is held together by His word. Anything contrary to His word leads to death. The pleasure, joy, and peace man seeks outside of God are only temporary, and will ultimately lead to death.

Repeatedly throughout the Bible, God reveals that the path to true well-being is in obedience to His word. We quote Deuteronomy 5:29 again to emphasize the intent of God's heart behind His commandments for His people:

> Oh, that they had such a heart in them that they would fear Me and always keep all My commandments, *that it might be well with them and with their children forever*! —(Emphasis added.)

Notice that the only reason God wanted the Israelites to obey His word was *"that it might be well with them and with their children forever!"*

The Lesson of Obedience Through Suffering

Implied in Deuteronomy 5:29 quoted above is the notion that our obedience to the word of God releases the blessing intended by God for us. But we should also remember what we learned in Chapter 3 about Lamentation 3:38, which says *that "Both bad and good things come by the command of the Most High God"* (ICB). An obvious conclusion emerges from the above two scriptures: that bad things—curses—also follow our disobedience of God's word.

Unfortunately, man cannot see the peril of disobeying the word of God until it is too late. Therefore God, out of love, must teach him obedience, so that it is forever engraved in his soul. Suffering is the tool that God uses to engrave in us the lessons of obedience to His word. I know this is hard for many to accept, but before I explain what I mean, let me define the suffering that God uses, lest people equate every pain and suffering to godliness.

God does not make you sick to teach you a lesson about healing. God does not deliberately kill your loved one to make you learn a lesson. Sickness or pain or death comes about for various reasons, and the devil is not responsible for all of them either. The truth is that, because man has freedom of choice, he also shares in the responsibility of life outcomes.

Nonetheless, it would be accurate to say that God may use the occasion of suffering, regardless of its source, to instruct us and to reveal His glory to us at different levels and in different dimensions. The sufferings God typically uses to mold obedience in us are what we may call, for lack of a better vocabulary, *pressures of life*. Moses told the Israelites in the wilderness:

> So [God] humbled you, allowed you to hunger, and fed you with manna which you did not know nor did your fathers know, that He might make you know that man shall not live by bread alone; but man lives by every *word* that proceeds from the mouth of the LORD — (Deuteronomy 8:3).

The carnal man, because of self-love, despises suffering. On the contrary, the truly spiritual person does not love his or her life unto death, because he or she sees suffering as a gateway to life. Paul shows in Romans 8:17 that, if we suffer with Jesus, we will also be glorified with him.

But why does God use suffering? Because, there is such a dire consequence to disobeying God's word at a certain level of spiritual life that God cannot afford to bring anyone to that level without being properly conditioned. This is the reason God seldom speaks to man directly, and mostly through other men or angels. In fact, this was why God wanted to designate an angel to go with the Israelites, when it became obvious they were going to have problems obeying His word in their journey to the Promised Land.

This was God edict in Exodus 33:3, *"Go up to a land flowing with milk and honey; for I will not go up in your midst, lest I consume you on the way, for you are a stiff-necked people."* We should never lose sight of the fact that God is both a loving father and a just Judge. In judgment, He is described as a *consuming fire* (see Hebrews 12:29). And Hebrews 10:31 adds *"It is a fearful thing to fall into the hands of the living God."*

This is not to paint God in a negative light. His grace is sufficient for all our shortcomings. Nevertheless, the fact remains that God's word out of His mouth is His very essence, and carries His full power behind it, as we learned in Chapter 3. Therefore, whoever receives the word of God assumes a great responsibility to handle that word with all diligence.

Isaiah 55:11 says that the proceeding word of God shall not return to Him void, but it shall accomplish the purpose for which God sent it. Accordingly, God will fulfill His word, either through us, when we obey, or over on top of us, when we disobey!

When God's word leaves His mouth, it cannot be reversed or altered. His word is his oath and he cannot reverse it once spoken. Ecclesiastics 8:4 is emphatic: *"... the word of the king is supreme"* — RSV. The New Century translation reads, *"What the King says is law."*

The Bible abounds with illustrations showing the supremacy of the word of the king. We learn of several kings that spoke rashly with their mouth, and had to pay deathly consequences, because they could not reverse their word once it was released (see for example Daniel 6:1-28). How much more established is the word of the King of the universe! *"Forever, oh Lord your word is settled in Heaven"* is the proclamation in Psalm 119:89. Because God's word is settled, it cannot be revoked.

It is this element of irrevocability of God's word that demands that, once the word of God is released, it must achieve an effect one way or the other. Our response to the word determines what effect the word will produce in the earth or in our lives. Obedience will be rewarded, and every disobedience will be crushed.

It is critical that we establish this point firmly in our mind and spirit: That God will not do any thing beyond or in contradiction to His word. We know that, *"God is love"* and *"his mercy endures forever"*, but both of these attributes of God are constrained by his word. Dire emergency, frantic begging, total remorse and, let me add, great intentions and works of righteousness will not move the love or mercy of God on your behalf except they harmonize with His word. On the other hand, if God speaks to you, and you obey by faith, then no matter how despicable you are, or how unspeakable your sins have been, God will move heaven and earth to help you.

It is very clear from what we have said so far that God does not take exceptions to His word. God does nothing without His word (see John 1:3), and He does not expect us to act any different. Therefore, walking in the light of God's word is not an option for the believer.

We can never achieve dominion in the earth without the word of God. So for us to ignore God's word in our lives speaks to our ignorance of God. And lacking knowledge of God, the majority of Christians have settled for a powerless, defeated life, living far below the privileges of their inheritance in Christ.

Hear God's warning again: *"...Watch out, you who live in your own light and warm yourselves by your own fires. This is the reward you will receive from me: You will soon lie down in great torment"* (Isaiah 50:11—NLT). And let us heed His plea to us in Isaiah 2:5: *"Come, people of Israel, let us walk in the light of the LORD!"*

God is pleading with us to walk in His light because we are His witnesses in the earth—the evidence of His goodness to the entire unbelieving world. We are also the evidence of His manifold wisdom to all the devils. God, in His infinite wisdom, is staking His credibility on us; and He will accomplish His purpose through us, one way or the other. But what abundant life awaits those who abide in His word continually to produce fruits that bring glory to Him!

We have repeatedly demonstrated the heart of God towards His people. God has made available every provision for us to live fulfilling lives here on earth. He has blessed us with every spiritual blessing in the heavenly places (Ephesians 1:3). He has given us everything that pertains to life and godliness, so we can share in His divine nature (2 Peter 1:3). And He has given us His Spirit so we can know the things He has freely given us (1 Corinthians 2:12). Therefore, if the promise of abundant life is eluding us, it is because we are walking in a light other than the light of God's word.

Interestingly however, many people are quickly disappointed in God when things go sour in their lives. I have even seen people get angry with God, lamenting why they are not as blessed as God promised, and recounting all the good works they do for Him. They suggest, in so many words, that somehow God has been unfaithful to them even though they have been faithful.

This is the absolute truth: The word of God cannot fail. So if you believe you are living by the word of God and experiencing constant defeat, then begin to question your understanding of God's word to you. The word of God is not subject to private interpretation according to 2 Peter 1:20. That is why God gave us the Holy Spirit, who would lead us into all truth and show us all things God has freely given us. Almost all of God's promises carry some conditions for their fulfillment, and virtually all the conditions are demands for actions and attitudes that prove our faith in God.

Yet the real problem is that many Christians filter the promises of God and ignore most of the conditions attached to the fulfillment of those promises. For instance, Psalm 103 is filled with rich promises and the assurance of the faithfulness of God, and what a delight to read and be satisfied that God has indeed taken care of all our problems. But verses 17 and 18 establish the condition for possessing these blessings.

> But the mercy of the LORD is from everlasting to everlasting on *those who fear Him*, and His righteousness to children's children, *to such as keep His covenant, and to those who remember His commandments to do them.*

In verses 20 and 21 of the same Psalm, we learn that even the angels are declared to be powerful only because they "Do His word... Heed the voice of His word...Do His pleasure." Also, in Psalm 91, a favorite Scripture in times of trouble, the promise of safety and protection are available to only those who abide in the secret place of the Most High, and who know the power of God's name. Christ also conditioned our receiving answers to prayer to abiding in Him and His words abiding in us (see John 15)

So let us add to our previous understanding regarding why believers go through sufferings. We have to distinguish between the sufferings we experience as a result of living in disobedience to the word of God and the sufferings that come with the testing of our faith, which the Lord allows from time to time for the purpose of spiritual growth. Job's case was a perfect example of a righteous man whose sufferings were orchestrated by God to bring Job into a higher spiritual dimension.

At the end Job's trial, we see the effect of this spiritual promotion through his own confession: *"I have heard of You by the hearing of the ear, but now my eye sees You"* (Job 42:5). Job moved from being just acquainted with God to having a clear vision of who God was. That was promotion.

And as if God wanted to assure us that the suffering He allows to come upon us, as believers, is indeed for our benefit, He caused Christ to learn obedience through sufferings, as shown in Hebrews 5:8— *"So even though Jesus was God's Son, he learned obedience from the things he suffered"* (NLT).

What is the point to all this? We are trying to establish beyond every reasonable doubt that it is impossible for the word of God to fail. Therefore, we can hang our very lives on God's word without fear. This is the assurance that faith gives us when God speaks to us.

To lean on our own understanding, trying to figure out life's decisions without God is a clear message of our faith in God. We are saying to God, we do not know Him well enough to trust Him with all of our heart. But if we understand that God's way is the only sure way, then seeking the will of God in all circumstances would become a life and death matter to us and not just a part-time activity.

As we discovered in Chapter 4, there is tremendous power resident in our soul by which we are able to accomplish incredible feats, even in our fallen adamic state. Consequently, we also discovered, there is a temptation for us to be oblivious to our need for God, and for us to make life decisions without God's authority. But we have learned that ignoring the word of God and leaning on our own understanding in making life decisions has dismal consequences, which robs us of the abundant life that defines God's kingdom. Knowing this, it becomes clear that our primary disposition in life, as believers, should be exactly what Proverbs 3:5 says:

> Trust in the LORD with all your heart; do not depend on your own understanding. Seek his will in all you do, and he will direct your paths—NLT

CHAPTER 7

FAITH COMES BY HEARING... THE WORD OF GOD

Thus far, we have established that the word that proceeds out of God's mouth is the greatest thing in the universe because it is the very essence of God Himself; and it represents His authority. Moreover, the entire Universe was birthed and is sustained by the word of God. Therefore, nothing exists outside of the word, and anything that appears contrary to the word of God will ultimately cease to exist.

By the same powerful word, God created man and appointed him to have dominion in the earth. It is logical to presume, therefore, that man's very existence and success on this earth would have something to do with his relationship with the word of God. And it does.

As we saw in Chapter 3, the principle of the oneness of God's word demands that, for man to achieve full dominion in the earth, his actions must conform to every word that proceeds from the mouth of God. Consequently, man's ability to *hear* and apply the word of God is crucial to him fulfilling this mandate of dominion in the earth.

We also learned in Chapter 4 that the blessing of dominion was given to all men regardless of their spiritual status. We further noted that the tree of the knowledge of good and evil represented man's effort to achieve dominion without God's authority. In that path, man was considered dead because he was disconnected from the word of life that birthed him.

Yet even in his fallen state, man retained his potential to have dominion, because his dominion capacity was connected to who he was rather than what he did or did not do. Therefore, the fall of man did not extinguish his ability to exercise dominion, even though it did diminish his effectiveness to maintain dominion.

The result of this inconsistency is a mixed blessing of tremendous progress in the face of insurmountable problems that man experiences in the world today. To eliminate this contradiction in his life, man has to *hear* from God, agree with what God says, and to move at the impulse of what God said. This is the only way man can achieve complete dominion in the earth.

From the above understanding, we can identify three important components needed for man to achieve complete dominion in the earth:

• The word proceeding out of the mouth of God
• Hearing the proceeding word of God
• Acting in accordance with the proceeding word

All of these components become increasingly defined in a life style of complete dependence on God, without which man's dominion in the earth is impossible, as we discussed in the last two chapters.

It is my belief that the most critical component is the ability to hear from God consistently. I single *hearing* out not because the other components are any less important. In fact, if we were to talk about the order of importance, we would say that the word out of God's mouth is the most important factor, because without it there would be no universe, no earth and nothing to dominate.

However, I consider *hearing* critical because it is the hardest skill to master; hence, it is often the missing piece to achieving complete dominion in the earth. Besides, we cannot act in accordance with God's word if we cannot hear what He says.

Starting from this chapter, therefore, we begin to explore the concept of *hearing* from God. Previously, we took for granted the idea of *spiritual hearing* in order to avoid overloading the reader with competing issues of equal importance. Furthermore, it was necessary first to understand the indispensability of the word of God in the universe in order to make obvious man's need to hear from God. I hope we accomplished that goal in the last three chapters.

We therefore turn our attention to this critical subject of spiritual hearing. But, to understand what it means to hear from God, we must first understand the concept of *time* from God's perspective. And here is why:

The Timelessness of God's Word and the Illusion of Time

God has already spoken. Or rather, God is yet speaking. You see, God is not moving through *time* as we know it on earth. Time, as we experience it on earth, is an earthly illusion caused by the rotation of the earth on its axis and its revolution around the sun.

Each of the other planets in the solar system has different measures of time due to differing rotational speeds and revolutions around the sun. So *time* is a very subjective concept the meaning of which depends on where you stand in the universe.

For instance, it takes 24 hours to make a day and 365.25 days to produce a year on earth. But measured in earth times, it takes 11.86 years to produce a year on Jupiter. On the other hand, a day on Venus is as long as 243 earth days (close to one year on earth). And strangely, a day on Venus is actually longer than a Venus year. In other words, it takes Venus longer to achieve a full rotation on its axis than it does one revolution around the sun!

Also, there are no seasons on either Mercury or Venus. Seasons are produced by the tilt of a planet towards the sun. However, Mercury does not tilt at all, whilst Venus tilts only so slightly (3 degrees compared to the 23 1/2 degrees tilt of the earth)—not enough to produce seasons.

What is the significance of this brief astronomy? We have established that days and seasons are phenomena of the rotation, the relative distance and tilt of the earth from the sun. So, if it were possible to stand on the sun, what would a day or a year look like? They would be meaningless concepts, or concepts with entirely different meanings from what we understand them to be on earth. On the sun, a day could be the same as a year and the same as a thousand years, depending on its own dynamics of movement.

So God, who sits outside of the universe, beholding everything in the universe at the same time, does not move through time the way we do on earth. The past, the present and the future are all one before God. He dwells in the ever-present day. A day is as a thousand years and a thousand years as a day in the eyes of God, according to 2 Peter 3:8. Revelations 21:25 illustrates this concept of timelessness in the City of God that comes to the earth, and has one continuous day that does not end.

This notion of timelessness in God's economy leads to a wonderful conclusion for all believers: Whatever we understand God to be saying to us today was spoken by God long before we arrived on this planet. In other words, when we hear God speak, it is not that He just started speaking, but that our spiritual ears just became attuned to what He has already said or has been saying.

This understanding also explains the concept of *revelation*. Revelation suggests that the thing being revealed already existed but was hidden from view or understanding.

The Timelessness of Faith

Knowing this concept should propel our faith to the heavens! Every word we need from God to succeed has already been spoken in Heaven. Every provision we need for life has already been granted by Him. We only need to hear what God has already said about our situation, and align our confession and action with what He said. The truth is, in heaven, the word of God has always been present; on earth, the word is proceeding and is manifesting itself in times and seasons.

Considered from another perspective, we can say that the word of God represents existing spiritual realities that are manifesting in the earth according to set times and seasons. Because time is inconsequential in the spirit realm, everything we hope to obtain from the spirit in a future period already exists now. Our ability to know these invisible realities and to cause them to become visible in the present is what living faith is all about.

Thus, the essence of faith is the ability to transcend time and to be assured of things that exist in the spirit but are not yet manifested. Walking by faith then is traversing the unseen world, and being able to bring into manifestation those spiritual realities we are assured of. Since it is solely a walk in the spirit, our natural senses are inadequate to help us. In fact, our natural senses become liabilities in the spirit, when they are assigned improper roles in our lives. Hence, *"...we walk by faith, not by sight"* (2 Corinthians 5:7).

The problem is that we are so used to living in *time* that a concept like this is bound to produce confusion. So let me use some examples from the Bible to illustrate how our faith can benefit from this understanding.

In Matthew 12:3, the Pharisees criticized Jesus for violating the Sabbath law, when he allowed his disciples to pluck ears of corn and eat them on a Sabbath day. Jesus responded by referring to David's actions in 1 Samuel 21:6, where David obtained consecrated showbread from Ahimelech the priest, and gave it to his hungry warriors to eat. The trouble was, under the Mosaic Law, it was unlawful for anyone other than a priest to eat such holy bread.

So the question becomes, why was David able to get away with this clear violation of God's law? We saw in the previous chapter how Uzzah died because he touched the Ark of the Covenant in violation of the Law (2 Samuel 6:6). And we also know from Acts 10:34 that God is no respecter of persons. So how do we reconcile these two different responses from God for the apparent violation of His law?

The answer is, David obtained and ate the showbread by faith. David saw by faith that the showbread represented the body of Christ that would be broken up to save men from death. Although the time of Christ was not yet come, David's faith brought the benefit of that future event into his time, and he did eat the holy bread with his men to save their lives and his from hunger.

The truth is, the body of Christ that was going to be broken for the salvation of men was already an accomplished fact in Heaven, even during David's time. This is why the Scriptures speak of Christ as the Lamb that was slain *from the foundations* of the world (see

Revelation 13:8). And this fact is what David, through revelation, understood and brought its benefit into his time.

According to Hebrews 11:1, David's revelation represents the essence of faith: the assurance of things hoped for, the evidence of things not seen. David's action of faith caused the invisible reality of the benefit of Christ's sacrifice to become evident in David's time. Even though it was not yet time on earth, in God's economy, it had always been time for man to be saved. David, therefore, transcended the limitations of earthly time, which we have demonstrated to be a mere illusion, to acquire the benefit of a future event.

Hence, we conclude that faith looks at things that are not yet manifested as though they were. This is exactly how God also sees things according to Romans 4:6. That is why it requires faith to walk with God. And that is why Enoch pleased God, and Abraham became a friend of God! Amos 3:16 says, *"How can two walk together except they be agreed?"* Said another way, how can we agree with God if we do not see the way He sees? Accordingly, Hebrews 11:6 says it is impossible to please God without faith. A lot of God's children are waiting for a better life some day in the future but, by faith, everything we are going to enjoy in Christ is available now, even if in a limited measure.

Here is another example from John 2:1-11. This is the story of Jesus turning the water into wine at a marriage feast. What is interesting in the story is the fact that when Mary asked Jesus to do something about the shortage of wine, Jesus replied that His time had not yet come. And yet Mary ignored that excuse and instructed the servants to go ahead and do whatever Jesus told them to do.

Mary's action was an act of faith. She knew by prophetic insight that Jesus was the Son of God. And if he truly was God's Son, then earthly time had no consequence on his power. In God's economy, every day—past, present or future—is 'Today'. Every time is a good time to experience the power of God. Mary stumbled upon this secret about faith and compelled Jesus to produce his first recorded miracle, even though he was reluctant to do so.

The best illustration of the concept we are discussing here is found in John 11:1-40, where Jesus raised Lazarus from the dead.

Let us dramatize the conversation between Jesus and Martha in this Scripture to highlight the subtle nuances in the story:

> *Martha:* "Lord, if you had been here, my brother would not have died. But even now I know that whatever you ask of God, God will give you."
> *Jesus:* "Your brother will rise again."
> *Martha*: "I know that he will rise again in the resurrection at the last day."
> *Jesus*: "**I am the resurrection and the life**. He who believes in me, though he may die, he shall live. And whoever lives and believes in me shall never die. Do you believe this?"

Martha had enough faith to believe that Jesus was the Messiah Israel had been waiting for. She also had enough faith to believe the promises of God regarding the Messiah. But, like most of us, she relegated God's promises to the future, when Christ would come in His glory.

Jesus corrected Martha, and emphatically revealed that his death and resurrection was already an accomplished fact in the spirit. He declared, "*I am the resurrection*", even though the event of his death and resurrection was in a future date! All Martha needed was faith to make this spiritual benefit manifest in her present circumstance.

Nevertheless, Martha's faith was still caught in the 'time-warp' we all struggle with sometimes. Her mind could not grasp what Jesus had just told her:

> *Jesus*: "Take away the stone."
> *Martha*: "Lord, by this time there is a stench, for he has been *dead* four days."
> *Jesus*: "Did I not say to you that if you would believe you would see the glory of God?"

Again, Jesus redirected her faith to focus on the spiritual reality that was about to manifest in the earth.

Like Martha, many of us believe in the promises of God, but we are all too prone to relegate any of those promises which cannot fit into our brains to a future setting. I repeat without any reservations: by faith, everything we are going to enjoy in the future glory is available now, even if in a limited measure! And I ask you the same question Jesus asked Martha: *"Do you believe this"* (John 11:25)? The next section explains why you should:

Faith Focuses Only On Invisible Realities

We can also describe faith as: gaining insight into the will of God concerning a situation, and taking action to cause the situation to conform to God's will. Faith focuses solely on unseen realities. It does not consider the past or what is visible in the present. It deals only with invisible things that are present with God, who also is invisible.

This does not imply that faith is oblivious to visible realities. Rather, it does not consider what it sees in the natural as having any value. Faith understands that what is seen is subject to what is not seen, because what is seen was birthed by what is not seen (implied by Hebrews 11:3).

The notion that visible realities have no value in the eyes of faith is what Abraham demonstrated, according to Romans 4:17-21. Verses 19 through 21 state in part: *"He did not consider his own body already dead…and the deadness of Sarah's womb…being fully convinced that what [God] had promised He was also able to perform."* Both Abraham's body and Sarah's womb were dead by all considerations, but Abraham's faith devalued those visible facts. Instead, it looked solely to the invisible realities of God's faithfulness and power to cause the visible facts to line up with God's word.

All the giants of faith listed in Hebrews 11 had one thing in common: they all looked to the invisible things of God—His promise, His faithfulness and His power—rather than the circumstances they faced. And in keeping their eyes on the invisible things of God, they obtained incredible miracles that made them appear super-humans.

Notice, however, what Hebrew 11:39 says about those men and women of faith: Although they all obtained a good testimony, they did not receive the promise. This implies that they lived their entire lives by faith, focused only on the invisible things of God. Every miracle they received birthed new aspirations of greater things in God. Every victory they achieved opened new doors of conquest to them. They were convinced of the unsearchable riches of God, and never limited God to what they could see with their natural eyes.

Therefore, the life of faith is not what many Christians make it to be: the one time exertion of spiritual energy to overcome a particular difficulty, and then to revert back to life as usual. No, overcoming faith is a lifestyle, rather than a tactical spiritual weapon that is invoked only in special times of need. *"The just shall live by faith"* (Romans 1:17) is the command of God, and Hebrew 10:38 adds to that Scripture, *"But if anyone draws back, My soul has no pleasure in him."* God does not want us to draw back from walking in faith at anytime.

Many who are suddenly in need of a miracle, find that faith is illusive when engaged only occasionally. Whereas those who walk consistently by faith find that miracles are only a by-product of the life of faith, and not the focus of it. But we cannot claim to *walk* by faith without *hearing* the word of God, because the basis for our faith is in what God has said to or about us.

Time According to Faith

After demonstrating earlier that faith is timeless, it appears somewhat contradictory to begin to talk about "time according to faith". Nevertheless, faith has a time, and it is 'now'. Faith always deals with the present. In the eyes of faith, the past is irrelevant, and the future exists only in the realm of hope. The present is the only reality faith recognizes.

Any believer who does not understand this concept is bound to meet with confusion and frustration in his or her faith walk. In fact, many believers have given up on their faith walk because of the lack of understanding of this concept. But remember Jesus' word in Mark 9:23: *"If you can believe, all things are possible to him who believes"*.

Let us try to discover the time dynamics of faith from a story in Mark 11:12-24, where Jesus cursed a fig tree. In that story, Jesus had cursed the fig tree in full view of his disciples the day before. The

very next day, as they walked by the tree, the disciples were aston-
ished to see that the fig tree had already withered because of the
curse. Jesus casually walked past the tree, as if nothing significant
had happened, which prompted Peter to call Jesus' attention to the
miracle: *"Rabbi, look! The fig tree which you cursed has withered
away"* (Mark 11:21).

Why was Peter amazed, but Jesus indifferent? After all a spectacular miracle had just taken place. The answer is in the statement
Jesus made to Peter:

> Have faith in God. For assuredly, I say to you,
> whoever says to this mountain, 'Be removed and be
> cast into the sea,' and does not doubt in his heart,
> but believes that those things he says will be done,
> he will have whatever he says. Therefore I say to
> you, whatever things you ask when you pray, *believe
> that you receive* them, *and you will have* them (Mark
> 11:22-24—emphasis added).

Jesus was not surprise to see that the fig tree had withered,
because he *saw* it withered immediately he cursed it; he *saw* it with
the eye of faith. If there were any praise or rejoicing to do over the
miracle, Jesus would have already done that the previous day, as
soon as he cursed the tree. According to faith, the curse took place
as soon as Jesus spoke over the tree. To the disciples, the curse took
effect the next day, when they saw the tree withered.

Now Jesus explains in v.24 of Mark 11, *"Therefore I say
to you, whatever things you ask when you pray, **believe that you
receive them**, and **you will have them."*** The point is, unless, we are
able to *see* the answer we are praying for as soon as we pray, we will
not see it come into manifestation.

Why is this the case? The answer is that, the evidence of faith is
not in the result we seek. Rather, it is in the word of God we *hear*. In
other words, when God speaks, His word, by itself, is the evidence
of the result we are seeking. This is because it is impossible for God
to speak and for His word to fail to produce the results intended.
This conviction is the basis for our assurance in God's faithfulness.

Therefore, Isaiah 55:10-11 says that, when God speaks, His word will accomplish the purpose God intended. Numbers 23:19 also says that God is not a man that He would lie—If God said it, He will do it!

Now it becomes obvious why Jesus instructed the disciples, in Mark 11:22, to put their faith in God, if they wanted to move mountains. Because, if their faith was based on what God has promised, then they were guaranteed success each time.

The assurance of faith, therefore, is in the fact that God has spoken, and He cannot go back on His word (Isaiah 45:23). It is this assurance that caused Sarah to receive strength to conceive Isaac. According to Hebrew 11:11, Sarah judged God faithful to fulfill His promise to them.

Now is also obvious why we have to hear from God to be able to walk by faith. Because, walking by faith is essentially walking according to the promises of God. Any motivation for action that is not based in the word of God is mere vanity or a dangerous presumption.

Action Alone Empowers Faith

Let us make an adjustment here before we go any further. Faith does not require righteousness to work. In other words, genuine faith is not the result of being righteous. Rather, faith produces righteousness in the person exercising it. Hence the Scripture: *"Abraham believed God, and it was accounted to him for righteousness"* (Genesis 15:6). This is to say that any person exercising faith can expect God's blessing, whether that person is a believer or not.

In fact, the sufficient condition for the word of God to work in a person's life is for that person to put God's word into action. Therefore, taking action in line with the word of God will produce the blessing the word promises, whether a person's faith is great or not. This is because faith is empowered through action taken in line with the word of God.

The story of Naaman in 2 Kings 5 affirms this principle. When the prophet Elisha told Naaman to go and dip seven times in the Jordan River for his healing, Naaman was skeptical. But when he eventually obeyed the prophet's word, he was miraculously healed of his leprosy. Naaman's pride, skepticism and reluctance did not prevent the word of God from producing the healing miracle when Naaman performed the required action. In other words, Naaman's action alone was responsible for activating the power of God's word to produce the miracle.

Even if we did not hear God speak, and accidentally fulfill the requirements of the spoken word, we could still be candidates for the blessing that comes with the word. An example from 2 Kings 7 illustrates this belief:

The word of the Lord came to Elisha, promising to end the famine in Samaria, which was under military siege by Syria. There were four lepers sitting outside of the city gate, who did not hear this word of the Lord, but whose thoughtful action, lining up with the promise of God, triggered a miraculous end to the siege, and turned the famine into a time of abundance. In this case, a timely action in line with the word of God was the sufficient condition for that word to be fulfilled.

In Biblical typology, leprosy is the condition of sin. Therefore, the four lepers outside the gate of Samaria typified sinners that are shut out of the kingdom of God due to their sin condition. Yet those were the same people whom God used to activate the power in His word to trigger a miraculous deliverance and provision for the City of Samaria. This story also adds to a point we made earlier about faith and unbelievers: that the word of God works for believers and unbelievers alike.

Let us consider one more thing regarding the word *action* as it relates to faith. When we speak of *action* in line with the word of God, we are not restricted to *doing* a *physical* activity only; but the *attitude* of a person also counts as action. Sometimes, refraining from taking a particular course of action because of what God has said is an action that empowers faith. In some other situations, just standing still and confessing the word of God is action enough to empower faith.

According to Romans 10: 9-10, a person is saved by believing in the heart and confessing with the mouth. In this case, confession with the mouth is the action required to empower belief in the heart to secure salvation. Thus, action is more of a heart attitude first, rather than a mere physical activity.

Nevertheless, I must add that virtually all faith actions will involve or demand an outward expression of some form of a physical action. James 2:18 says: *"But someone will say, 'You have faith, and I have works.' Show me your faith without your works, and I will show you my faith by my works."* James explains that, when we read in the Scriptures that God attributed righteousness to Abraham because he believed Him, Abraham's faith was shown to be genuine when he was willing to offer his son, as God had demanded. Accordingly, in verse 22 of James 2, we read: *"Do you see that faith was working together with his works, and by works faith was made perfect."*

If we truly believe in something, our belief will affect our attitudes and actions. Belief that leads to action is genuine faith. One preacher describes belief that leads to action as *persuasion*. It is only when we are persuaded that we would be willing to take action. In fact, the strongest assurance of faith will have zero effect, if not accompanied by a corresponding action. Hence the Scripture: *"... Faith without works is dead"* (James 2:20).

Why is Faith Neutral?

In the Story of Naaman and the four lepers outside the gates of Samaria, we learned that faith and the word of God work for unbelievers as well. But how can unbelievers benefit from God's word even though they do not have a part in God's Kingdom? They can because, as we saw in Chapter 3, the word of God regulates and upholds everything in the universe (see also Hebrews 1:3). Psalm 103:19 says that Gods kingdom rules over all things.

Consequently, when the word of God enters into the earth realm, it is available to all men— *"For He makes His sun rise on the evil and on the good, and sends rain on the just and on the unjust"* (Matthew 5:45). Whoever, therefore, will fulfill the requirement of the word, whether by faith or by providence, will receive the promise of the word.

To further elaborate the point made here, let us look at Hebrews 11:3: *"By faith we understand that the **worlds** were framed by the word of God."* The Greek word, *aion,* translated *world* is also *ages.*

Included in the meaning of this Scripture is the notion that God has demarcated periods of time called *ages*, when certain events and dispensations would occur in the earth. These periods are outside of man's control. Events earmarked for a particular age will occur regardless of what man does, even though, historically, God has always prepared someone for the set time to fulfill His will.

The Scriptures say that it was the word of God that framed these ages. A synonym of the word *frame* is *border,* implying that God's word is revealed in the earth at set times to mark off the completion of one period and the beginning of another. In other words, during a specific age, a specific word of God is revealed to govern that period. Whoever, through faith or providence, walks in line with that word for that particular period receives the blessing of the word for that age. Believers as well as unbelievers can benefit from that word, if their actions correspond to the requirement of the word for that age. It is therefore not surprising that a lot of discoveries in the world that have benefited the gospel of Christ came not by believers but by unbelievers.

Hence, we conclude that faith is a phenomenon for all men, believers and unbelievers alike. Virtually all of the people who received special commendations from Jesus about having great faith were neither disciples of Jesus, nor part of the religious elite of the day. We may characterize the centurion in Matthew 8:5, the woman with the issue of blood in Luke 8:43, and the Syrophenician woman in Mark 7:28 as unbelievers. But they all exhibited faith that earned commendations from Jesus. Indeed, as the stories of those unbelievers suggest, anyone who is convinced about a cause, and invests all efforts to realize that cause is demonstrating faith.

Faith runs the world. Without faith, there would be very little progress in the world. All the systems that have been built to make life work in this world depend on the faith of the people who use and make them work. We demonstrate faith when we give our monies to financial institutions for safekeeping. We demonstrate faith when we travel by airplane. The list can go on forever. The point is, we as Christians often talk about faith as if we own it, even though we are the least likely group of people to live by our faith.

Faith then is as neutral as money is in the world. Money takes its nature from the use it is put. Therefore, money becomes good or evil depending on what it is used for. Similarly, faith is either spiritual or natural depending on the use it is put.

Hence we have natural faith that drives systems in the world, and spiritual faith that controls things in the spirit. This is also one reason Jesus instructed the disciples to *"have faith in God"*, as we saw in Mark 11:22. For it is only with God that nothing is impossible; therefore, only faith in God could overcome deeply rooted problems, as Jesus was trying to teach them.

So what advantage has the believer who has faith then? Much in every way! Romans 10:17 says, *"Faith comes by hearing ... the word of God."* The believer has the advantage of hearing the word of God, and not merely bumping into it accidentally. As believers, we have the privilege of knowing we can always approach the throne of God boldly, and receive whatever we need (see Hebrews 4:16). James 1:5 also says that, whenever we lack wisdom, we can ask God, and He will freely give it to us. And whatever we hear from God becomes the key to victory in the situation we face.

"Without Faith It is Impossible To Please God"

The above subheading quoted from Hebrews 11:6 sets, in no uncertain terms, God's condition for man to relate to Him. Note that it does not merely say God is not pleased when we do not have faith. It says it is *impossible* to please Him without faith.

This scripture is emphasizing to us something we easily take for granted: that faith is not an option in the kingdom of God. Therefore, man cannot do anything of worth in the spirit without faith. If we put this concept alongside the notion that God will not do anything in the earth without His word, we come to the understanding that faith and the word of God are inseparable. Hence Romans 10:17 says, *"Faith comes by hearing... the word of God"*.

The question is why does God predicate our relationship with Him entirely upon faith? In order to answer this question, we need to grasp the significance of Isaiah 55:10-11, which we quote again below:

> For as the rain comes down, and the snow from
> Heaven, and do not return there, but water the earth,
> and make it bring forth and bud, that it may give seed
> to the sower and bread to the eater, so shall My word
> be that goes forth from My mouth; It shall not return
> to Me void, but it shall accomplish what I please, and
> it shall prosper in the thing for which I sent it.

In the above Scripture, God is declaring His word to be an absolute certainty. The word of God released in the earth (whether to an individual or a group of people) shall not fail to accomplish God's purpose in sending that word. But by God's own sovereign choice, He has delegated authority in the earth to man; therefore, God **must** work through man to accomplish His purpose in the earth.

We determined earlier that the word of God has always existed, and represents invisible realities in the spirit. We also understood that faith is the force that brings into manifestation those invisible realities in the spirit. So in order for God's word to be fulfilled in the earth, someone must act on it by faith. This is why the word of God comes with faith, to inspire a person to fulfill the word.

It is evident, therefore, why God insists on faith as the only means to please Him. For, without faith, God's purpose will not be accomplished in the earth. Perhaps, this also explains why, in any particular age, God reserves for Himself a remnant of people who would not conform to the corruption in that age. I believe God does this in order to preserve faith to accomplish His purpose in the earth.

Mixing the Word of God with Faith

From the foregoing section, it is clear that faith is automatically released when God's word comes to a person. It is the assurance one receives from the Holy Spirit that says, "This is possible; this is within reach". This is what we may call divine inspiration.

This assurance often comes in the face of contradicting circumstances, which compels the person who receives the word to decide whether to follow the assurance of the word, or to yield to the fear evoked by the contradicting circumstance. This is why Paul cautions us not to walk by sight but by faith (see 2 Corinthians 5:7).

As we learned earlier, the assurance of faith is totally useless if it does not lead to action in the believer. Hence, James 2:17: *"Thus also faith by itself, if it does not have works, is dead."* This was the problem of the liberated Israelites who failed to get to the Promised Land. Hebrew 4:2 says that, *"For indeed the gospel was preached to us as well as to them; but the word which they heard did not profit them, not being mixed with faith in those who heard it.*

So the word of God came to them; Faith also came to them by the word; but they failed to mix the word with faith. How did they fail? They complained, they murmured, they disobeyed, and finally, they concluded they were not able to do what God said they were able to do. So they failed to mix the word with faith in this sense: their confessions and actions were not affected by the word of God they had heard. Therefore, the word did not benefit them, and they all died in the wilderness outside the Promised Land.

This brings us back to our original statement: The sufficient condition for the word of God to work is action taken in line with the requirement of the word. Yes, believe in your heart, but then do something with what you believe. That is the power of the message, *"If you can believe, all things are possible to him who believes"* (Mark 9:23).

The Advantage of the Believer

What happens if the word of God does not find faith or agreement in a person? The word makes a way for itself. Since Isaiah 55:10 says that God's word shall not return to Him without accomplishing the purpose for which He sent it, God Himself sees to the fulfillment of the word (see Jeremiah 1:12). This is the reason God is able to promise the impossible, even though He uses men who have limitations and outright character flaws.

For instance, He tells Mary, a virgin, that she would have a child without a husband. Mary's reaction was, *"How can this be?"* God's response: *"With God nothing is impossible"* (Luke 1:37). In Isaiah 59:16, we read: *"Then the Lord saw it, and it displeased Him that there was no justice. He saw that there was no man, and wondered that there was no intercessor; Therefore **His own arm** brought salvation for Him; And **His own righteousness**, it sustained Him.*

119

It is clear that, when God cannot find a ready man, He begins to initiate actions that get the job done. God is reminding us over and again that, regardless of who or what He uses to accomplish His purpose, He is still the one in charge. This understanding illuminates the scripture: *"Not by might, nor by power, but by My Spirit, says the LORD of hosts"* (Zechariah 4:6).

The primary agent for fulfilling the word of God in the earth has always been the Holy Spirit. He was in the beginning the only agent for fulfilling God's purpose in the earth before man was created. And since man's creation, He still is the primary agent of God's purpose. But now, He accomplishes God's purpose in the earth through man because of man's authority to exercise dominion in the earth.

This is simply to remind us that man is never in full control of what happens in the earth. Man's dominion in the earth is a delegated authority, which implies that man is still subject to God. Proverbs 19:21 speaks to the same effect: *"There are many plans in a man's heart, nevertheless the Lord's counsel—that will stand"*. This Scripture puts the exclamation point to what we have been saying. Men can desire and design all sorts of plans, but, in the end, it is God's will that will be accomplished.

Therefore, when the word of God does not find a person or a people of faith, it begins to send signals through the visible environment. It begins to pressure everything in the environment until the environment begins to speak out—We understand the invisible things of God by what He makes visible in the earth (see Romans 1:19-20).

When the word of begins to send signals in the environment, anyone—believers and unbelievers alike—can observe and recognize a trend or a phenomenon unfolding within the environment. During this time, the Holy Spirit also begins to inject thoughts and imaginations of possibilities to inspire people to take purposeful action to fulfill God's will. Since understanding is mostly a mental activity, anyone with intelligence can understand and take action to fulfill the word, whether that person is a believer or not.

The phenomena of the printing press and the computer, for examples, were not man's ideas, but were birthed from heaven for the purpose of accelerating the establishment of the kingdom of God in the earth. If there had been believers who were sensitive and equipped enough to fulfill God's mandate, they could have tapped into those ideas in the spirit before they manifested in the visible world.

If we, as believers, allow God to open our ears to hear in the spirit, no phenomenon, whether good or bad, coming into the world should surprise us. It is this same privilege of fore-knowledge that enabled Joseph (Genesis 40) and Daniel (Daniel 2) to foresee events God had scheduled to come upon the earth in their times and beyond. Amos 3:7 says: *"Surely the Lord GOD does nothing, unless He reveals His secret to His servants the prophets."* Also, 1 Thessalonians 5:2 says that the day of the Lord will come as a thief in the night, and in verse four of the same Scripture, Paul reminds us: *"But you, brethren, are not in darkness, so that this Day should overtake you as a thief."*

In fact, the purpose of the Last Days outpouring of the Holy Ghost is to empower God's people to accelerate the establishment of the kingdom of God in the earth. The effect of this empowerment is, in part, to supernaturally heighten the intelligence and imaginations of God's people. Hence, Joel 2:28 says: *"And it shall come to pass afterward that I will pour out My Spirit on all flesh; your sons and your daughters shall **prophesy**, your old men shall **dream** dreams, your young men shall **see visions**.*

Therefore, the critical challenge facing all believers in this hour is to have a spiritual ear to hear what God is saying in our time. And when we hear God speak, we should mix faith with what we hear to establish God's purpose in the earth. Nevertheless, God's word will come to pass with or without us, as believers.

The advantage the believer has is the in-dwelling Holy Ghost, who is here to guide us into all truths, and to show us things to come. If we wait until the word of God begins to exert influence in the visible environment, then we would have already lost the advantage in whatever blessing the word carries, because, by that time, the word of God would have become accessible to unbelievers too.

We reemphasize here that God, as the creator of all things in the universe, owns all things. Everything in the universe is a servant of God, including all mankind, holy angels and fallen angels, animals and plants and all inanimate objects, both visible and invisible. Jesus

121

said in Luke 19:40 that, even if men stopped praising God, the very stones would begin to cry out His praise. That everyone on earth is subject to God is the meaning communicated by Isaiah 45:23 — " *I have sworn by my own name, and I will never go back on my word: Every knee will bow to me, and every tongue will confess allegiance to my name"* (NLT).

Therefore, God can use anyone or anything that meets the criteria for fulfilling His word in the earth. But as we learned in Amos 3:7, God will reveal His word to His people first before He causes the word to manifest in the visible world. The question is, do we have the ear to hear the Word of God. And do we have the faith to establish the word when we hear it?

The Handicap of the Believer

We have already defined faith as an assurance and evidence of things that we cannot yet see. It is this assurance that compels us to take action in line with what we hear. This means that a believer who hears the voice of God will be able to access Heavenly benefits simply by exercising his or her faith. Unbelievers have no such privilege. They can only become aware of an unfolding phenomenon by observation and study, which becomes possible when the word begins to exert influence in the visible environment. Only then are unbelievers able to take appropriate action by their intellectual power.

In spite of their spiritual handicap, however, unbelievers appear to be more effective than believers in establishing their convictions in the earth. In Luke Chapter 16, Jesus tells a parable of an unjust steward. What is unexpected in that story is Jesus commending the action of the unjust steward. This was a man who had a mind to cheat his master for his own benefit; yet Jesus used him as an example to reprimand God's people.

The point Jesus was showing us was that, when the stewards learned of his master's intention to fire him, he took action to benefit from the impending misfortune rather than wait to become a victim of it. By the same token, since we, as believers, know all about God's intentions or promises for us in this age, we ought to be able to benefit from our foreknowledge.

Observe the tremendous progress unbelievers have accomplished in the world today. See how much they have profited from their limited abilities and knowledge. Now, compare that to what we profess God has given us in Christ, and how much of that inheritance we actually experience in the earth today. Jesus' statement is certainly true: *"The sons of this world are more shrewd in their generation than the sons of light"* (Luke 16:8).

What it Means to Walk by Faith or By the Word of God

Because faith is the only means by which we can accomplish God's will on earth, faith is not an option in the kingdom of God. And since faith comes by hearing the word of God, hearing and walking by the word of God is also not an option in the kingdom of God. (We have already determined in earlier chapters that God will never do anything apart from His word.)

Nevertheless, walking by faith does not mean that, for every detail of our lives, we have to wait for a specific word from God before we can make a decision, and take an action. If that was the case, then a person who walks by faith can accomplish very little in the world.

Typically, God releases a word to govern a particular season in our lives. He then requires us to live by that word during that season until He releases another word to us for the next season. So every decision we make and every action we take during a particular season ought to be molded or influenced by the revealed will of God for that season. If our decisions and actions are shaped by what God says to us in a particular season, then we are walking by faith and not by sight.

God gives us an illustration of this notion of walking by a particular word for a whole season in 1 Kings 19:8. In this Scripture, God fed Elijah a meal that enabled him to go in the strength of that meal for forty days and forty nights until he heard God's voice again. The principle is that, until we hear God's voice again, we should walk with the truth we already know.

In between the times God speaks to us, He guides our steps by His Spirit until we are ready for the next season of life. God does not want us to be passive or to sit idle, purportedly, waiting to hear His word before we can take action. This is what Psalm 32:9 admonishes us not to do. We will examine Psalm 32 in greater detail in the succeeding paragraphs to reinforce the understanding presented here.

God owns both the heavens and the earth, and yet he has given the administration of the earth to man (see Psalm 115:16). In the same way, He is both the Father of all spirits and the God of all flesh; yet, as to the administration of the flesh (natural), the responsibility lies with man.

We have already explored the notion that man is sovereign over his own destiny. It is this unique privilege that makes faith necessary, requiring man to choose to obey God, and to submit himself to God's will of his own free accord.

Therefore, in Psalm 32:8-9, we read:

> I will instruct you and teach you in the way you should go; I will guide you with My eye. Do not be like the horse or like the mule, which have no understanding, which must be harnessed with bit and bridle, else they will not come near you.

The above Scripture delineates the responsibilities of God as well as of man in the walk of faith. We learned in Chapter 4 that, under the New Covenant, God says we will know Him, because He will teach us directly by His Spirit in our heart. But because man has freedom of choice, he must choose to cooperate with God for God to step into his world. That is why Proverbs 3:5 says man *must* acknowledge God in all of his ways for God to direct him. As soon as man acknowledges God, God promises to teach him and direct his steps to success.

According to Psalm 32:8-9 quoted above, however, God is not going to necessarily speak to us on every turn for us to do anything. Rather, God says he will instruct us and teach us the way we should go, and then, He will *guide us with His eye*. This implies that, God will show us the master plan, teach us how to build it, and guide us to build it using the creativity of our own faith.

The end results of what we build will be directly related to what we can see by our faith. We are to build according to the Heavenly pattern He shows us; but how big or small the results turns out to be will depend on what we see by faith. Thus, because God has given man a measure of sovereignty, He is not going micro-manage every detail of man's life. God expects man to use faith to establish what He says to him for each season in life.

Herein also lies a great test for man: That is, for man to regard himself as a mere steward of God still subject to the word of God. Jesus is our example in this disposition. Philippians 2:5 says that, though Jesus was in his very nature God, he did not cling to that privilege but humbly submitted himself to the will of God.

The way we submit to God is by acknowledging God as our source in everything through prayer. When we do, God says He will instruct us and teach us the way we should go. This is why we learn in Proverbs 3:5, *"In all your ways acknowledge him and he will direct your path"*

Man should, therefore, seek to act in harmony with the will of God in exercising dominion in this world. The failure of Adam and Eve was in this very fact—They chose the possibility of achieving dominion in the earth without God. But the truth is, they were created to *represent* God on earth and not to *replace* Him. In contrast, listen to the heart of Jesus in the following Scriptures:

> "I assure you, the Son can do nothing by himself. He does only what he sees the Father doing. Whatever the Father does, the Son also does"—John 5:19.

> I can of Myself do nothing. As I hear, I judge; and My judgment is righteous, because I do not seek My own will but the will of the Father who sent Me" —John 5:30.

> When ye have lifted up the Son of man, then shall ye know that I am he, and that I do nothing of myself; but as my Father hath taught me, I speak these things"—John 8:28.

And here is the summary disposition of Christ, as man, which leads to complete dominion on earth, and which all believers are encouraged to emulate:

> Though he was God, he did not think of equality with God as something to cling to. Instead, he gave up his divine privileges; he took the humble position of a slave and was born as a human being. When he appeared in human form, he humbled himself in obedience to God and died a criminal's death on a cross. Therefore, God elevated him to the place of highest honor and gave him the name above all other names, that at the name of Jesus every knee should bow, in heaven and on earth and under the earth, and every tongue confess that Jesus Christ is Lord, to the glory of God the Father (Philippians 2:5-11—NLT).

So in our walk with God, we are at liberty to choose our own way, which leads to death. Or we can choose to acknowledge God in our plans for Him to guide or direct our steps, as He promises in Psalm 32 and Proverbs 3. Just as it was in the Garden of Eden, man still has the choice to eat from the tree of life or from the tree of the knowledge of good and evil.

The words, *guide* in Psalm 32:8 and *direct* in Proverb 3:6, are the keys to understanding what we have been saying so far. They speak of God not directly dictating details of what man must do, but ensuring that man's decisions and actions line up with God's will.

So God expects us to use our choices creatively to come up with a variety of ideas and inventions within the scope of His will. But, as we acknowledge Him, He leads us *"in the paths of righteousness"* (Psalm 23), wherein we achieve prosperity and good successes. This was the secret of King Uzziah. In 2 Chronicles 26:4, we learn that as long as Uzziah sought the Lord, he prospered—As long as he acknowledged God in his decisions, he received God's guidance, which brought him great success.

You Are Accountable Only For What You Hear

It is true to say that in the walk of faith, such as illustrated by the life of Abraham, God holds us accountable only for His will that He has revealed to us. So we can say Abraham walked in perfect harmony with the will of God in spite of several instances of failures he exhibited along his journey with God.

For instance, God directs him to leave his country; he leaves. He commands him to circumcise all male persons in his house; he complies. God instructs him to heed the voice of his wife, and send Ishmael away; he obeys. Then, in the ultimate test of faith, God demands that he sacrifices his son Isaac; and he is willing to do so. Each of these directives from God was difficult in its own respect, but nowhere in the Scriptures is it suggested that Abraham sought to bargain with God or question God's judgment. Abraham simply obeyed without questions.

Yet at the same time, in between this walk of faith, we see a weak and a fearful Abraham, even willing to trade his wife for personal security. We also see the father of faith doubting God's ability to give him a child past old age, and therefore, taking steps to fulfill the promise himself. The result of that unbelief was the saga of Ishmael we mentioned in Chapter 6.

Strangely, there is no record of God ever reprimanding Abraham for these blunders. As long as Abraham was on the move as God instructed him, he was in perfect harmony with God. In fact, in the encounter with Abimelech (Genesis 20:1-10), God threatened to kill Abimelech for taking Sarah to be his wife, even though it was Abraham's fault. It was Abimelech that received the rebuke not Abraham.

This is the principle: as long as we are walking in the revealed will of God, no matter how small our light is, our mistakes are not imputed unto us. The apostle John gives us a hint as to why this is the case in 1 John 1:8: *"if we walk in the light, as he is in the light… the blood of Jesus cleanses us from all unrighteousness."* The condition is *"if we walk in the light…"* What is this light? Psalm 119:105: *'Your word is … a light unto my path."*

So when the word of God comes to us, and we walk in it faithfully, God takes care of all that concern us. God becomes our righteousness and our perfection, when we believe and walk faithfully in His word. Abraham's righteousness before God was not because he was perfect, but because he believed God.

It is somewhat disappointing, however, to note that Abraham did not seek God about some of the critical decisions he made; and we know that those decisions resulted in grave consequences for the future. But because he faithfully obeyed the word of God that came to him, God imputed righteousness to him, and overlooked his failures. This is the good news God is communicating to us in Psalm 32:1-2:

> Blessed *is he whose* transgression *is* forgiven, w*hose*
> sin *is* covered. Blessed *is* the man to whom the Lord
> does not impute iniquity...

Hence, it is true that God has given us a measure of sovereignty as to how we govern our natural world. But He admonishes us to seek His wisdom, if all is to go well with us. Although, for the believer, everything ultimately turns out for good because of God's grace, we can avoid a lot of the pain we go through when we walk by our own understanding.

We should never forget that the fruit of the knowledge of good and evil always leads to death. True, God's gifts and calling are irrevocable (Romans 11:29); but alas, what curses we bring upon ourselves when we do not acknowledge God in all our ways!

Believers should be miles ahead of unbelievers in living victoriously in this world because of our capacity to hear from God. We should not be merely stumbling unto the promises of God, but we should be actively seeking those promises, and living by them to demonstrate God's goodness.

And beyond just demonstrating God's goodness, the knowledge of God's promises is what will enable us to share in the divine nature of God, according to 2 Peter 1:3-4. We will talk more about this subject in Chapter 8.

But the point is, we are the living witnesses God has in the earth. And what lousy witnesses we have been so far! What is our life saying about God's grace and goodness to man? Where is our evidence of the power of God's kingdom? Jesus taught us to pray in Luke 11:2, *"Your kingdom come. Your will be done on earth as it is in Heaven."* Knowing the will of God and establishing it in the earth by faith is how the kingdom of God will become evident to the world.

Since we are required to walk by faith, and faith comes by hearing the word of God, we should make an effort to hear from God. In fact, I believe the number one goal, if not the only goal, of every Christian should be to know the will of God, and to make it happen in the earth. Therefore, hearing from God should be our most significant quest in life, everyday. And when we do hear the word of God, we should not shrink back in unbelief, but by faith, establish God's will in the earth. God is relying on us and declares to us:

> "But you are my witnesses...!" says the LORD. "...You have been chosen to know me, believe in me, and understand that I alone am God. There is no other God; there never has been and never will be. I am the LORD, and there is no other Savior" (Isaiah 43:10-11—NLT).

But then Jesus asks: *"... when I, the Son of Man, return, how many will I find who have faith"* (Luke 18:8 —NLT)?

CHAPTER 8

SPIRITUAL HEARING

W e have demonstrated that we have to hear the word of God and walk by its light, if we are to fulfill our mandate of dominion in the earth. We have also shown that the word of God shall be fulfilled with or without believers. Hence, in order for us, as believers, to profit from God's word, we should accord it the highest priority in our lives. And for us to give God's word the priority it deserves, we have to be able to hear God's voice in the first place.

But what does it mean to hear from God? How does God speak to us? This is the point where many Christians run into confusion and misconceptions. Therefore, in this chapter, we delve into the mechanics of spiritual hearing, hoping to remove some of the misconception and abuse often surrounding this critical spiritual reality.

The Dangers of Spiritual Hearing

The subject matter of hearing from God is so fraught with dangers, so susceptible to deception, and so often abused that I introduce it here with great caution. For someone to claim to hear from God is for that person to also claim to know with certainty the voice of God. The problem is, there are many voices in the world, and each one of them is saying something (see I Corinthians 14:10).

131

Even our own body and soul talk to us, and we can easily mistake their sound as divine.

If we were knowledgeable about all the principles that govern the spirit world, spiritual life would be a science rather than an art. But alas, when it comes to spiritual life, we grope in the dark most of the time. We are like the proverbial ten blind men describing what an elephant looked like, each from his own point of touch. This is exactly what Paul meant in I Corinthians 13:12: *"Now we see things imperfectly as in a poor mirror, but then we will see everything with perfect clarity. All that I know now is partial and incomplete, but then I will know everything completely, just as God knows me now"* — NLT.

Our disadvantage of a fuzzy and partial knowledge of the spirit realm makes our experience of a spiritual phenomenon very subjective, and opened to diverse interpretations. That is why Satan has succeeded in becoming a master deceiver. He exploits the ignorance of men to his advantage, and I cannot imagine anyone, Christ apart, who has not fallen prey to his devious schemes at one time or another.

But God does speak to us, and He wants us to hear his voice in spite of the dangers. No relationship will survive long without an open communication channel going both ways. That tells me God must have a secure way for us to hear his voice without the potential for deception. He must have a way, because He is counting on us to establish His rule upon the earth. This is why Jesus taught us to pray for the will of God to be done on earth as it is done in Heaven.

To communicate the grand scheme of His will to us, God gave us the Holy Scriptures–the Bible. The dilemma is that the will of God in every life situation is not explicitly stated in the Bible. That is to say, we cannot always know the mind of God about every issue in life simply by reading the Scriptures. The Bible is very dynamic and lends itself to flexible interpretations, which some people have exploited throughout history for their own selfish ends. This is why we have to understand spiritual hearing.

To be faithful to a subject so controversial, I have chosen to stay very close to the Scriptures as far as practicable. But even here, my interpretations of what the Bible says about the subject cannot be entirely free from my own subjective experience of this phenomenon. Therefore, nothing here is prescriptive. The Holy Spirit himself is our designated teacher, who will lead us into all truth. As we come to know God more through our individual unique experiences with Him, He will reveal to us deeper understanding about this subject based on the level of maturity we have attained.

What does it mean to hear from God?

Let me first suggest that hearing the voice of God is not necessarily a physical activity. It is true that God sometimes speak to people in an audible voice. And this reality is not confined to the Old Testament believers alone. For we read in the Acts of the Apostles several instances where the Holy Spirit spoke audibly to some of the believers. But I believe the primary reason most of God's children cannot hear His voice is because they always expect to hear an *audible* voice.

To correct this misconception, let us take a peek into the spirit world, fuzzy as it may seem to us at this point: In the spirit world, everything *is* exactly as it appears—everything is naked. You cannot fake righteousness in the spirit. You cannot fake spiritual power or authority. You are instantly recognized by your spiritual worth in the spirit world. That is why the demons were able to recognize Jesus as He walked by (see Mark 3:11). That is why they were able to recognize the authority of Paul versus the lack of authority of the seven sons of Sceva in Acts 19:14-16.

Let us look at the spirit world from another perspective. When we speak, we can make people understand something different from what is in our heart. So our words may carry encouragement to a person whilst, in our heart, we carry judgment and criticism about that person. In the spirit, however, it is only our judgment and criticism that will be evident, not what we want people to hear or see. (Some Christians should take note and stop their spiritual hypocrisy.)

Hebrews 4:13 in speaking about God says: *"Nothing in all creation can hide from him. Everything is naked and exposed before his eye"*—NLT. This Scripture speaks of God's omniscient power or His ability to know all things. However, since God is the father of spirits (Hebrews 12:9), we can conclude that all spirits have a degree of this ability.

This does not necessarily imply that demons can read a person's thoughts, for instance. In my opinion and observation, demons can influence our thoughts by injecting ideas and imaginations to us. They can also manipulate an atmosphere to incline us to act or think a certain way. But demons cannot read our mind at will.

Psalm 39 says, *"I will keep my mouth with a bridle, while the wicked is before me."* In other words, as long as my intentions are in my thoughts, the devils or the ungodly have no access to that information. It is when we open our mouths that we give away what is in our heart.

Listen to Matthew 12:34-37 and be instructed:

> ...For out of the abundance of the heart the mouth speaks. A good man out of the good treasure of his heart brings forth good things, and an evil man out of the evil treasure brings forth evil things. But I say to you that for every idle word men may speak, they will give account of it in the day of judgment. For by your words you will be justified, and by your words you will be condemned.

It is obvious from the above Scripture why we have to put a bridle on our mouth, especially, when we are aware our enemy is listening. Putting a bridle on our mouths is not to keep us from speaking what is in our heart, but to ensure that we judge the appropriateness of what we are about to say before we say it.

So what is spiritual hearing? Spiritual hearing is not merely the sound and words we hear in our natural ear, but rather, the wisdom, the understanding or information we receive regarding a particular matter in the spirit. It is the reception of knowledge or an intuitive awareness about a subject without intellectual analysis. In other words, it is knowledge that manifests in us directly, while bypassing our intellectual or auditory faculties. The struggle to define spiritual hearing is due to its subjective nature. Nonetheless, it is a spiritual reality. In fact, it is a critical asset in our quest to walk with God. Let us explain further:

Spiritual Hearing versus Natural Intuition

Spiritual hearing is not the same as the natural intuition a person may sometimes receive regarding a particular matter. Every human being has a natural intuition. Exactly how intuition works is still a mystery, and no one has control over when and how to sense an intuition. Like spiritual hearing, it impinges directly with no apparent logic for it. We sometimes call intuition a *hunch* or a *gut feeling*. My own interpretation is that intuition is part of our yet-to-be-understood power of the soul, and it can be sharper in some people than in others.

There is also, however, an intuition that is the voice of our spirit. God speaks to us in our spirit, where He also resides. The major difference between spiritual intuition and natural intuition is that the spiritual encompasses the sense of the natural intuition and more. The reason this is the case is that our natural intuition is the vehicle for expressing what our spiritual intuition senses.

In fact, virtually every spiritual phenomenon that comes to us is experienced through our natural faculties. In this sense, our natural faculties only play a secondary role in the things of the spirit, and never a leading role. They are there to express and carry out what our spirit senses as the will of God.

Because spiritual hearing is not a product of the brain, sometimes it conflicts with natural intelligence. Typically, it takes a little more time for our intellect to grasp what we hear in our spirit. And if what we hear requires an action that appears contrary to natural wisdom, it may take a long time for our intellect to fully comprehend what we apprehended in our spirit.

Dangers in Spiritual Hearing

There are dangers in trying to follow the leading of one's spirit. Not all *sensing* or *hearing* comes from God. That is why the Bible cautions us not to believe every spirit, but to try the spirits to know if they are of God (see 1 John 4:1). We are to view any spiritual information we receive in the light of the Scriptures. Anything that directly conflicts with Scripture cannot be from the Spirit of God, and ought to be rejected instantly. Anything that does not have a direct backing of the Scriptures ought to be investigated further.

Hence, our knowledge of the word of God is a great asset in judging what is of God and what is not. Nevertheless, there is a vast array of life situations where the Scriptures do not offer specific guidance. In such instances, our relationship with the Holy Spirit and our maturity level would determine the type of guidance we get. Immature believers may not be able to judge spiritual things accurately. Therefore, they should consult with the particular spiritual authority over them before they undertake any major changes to their life that is the result of allegedly hearing from God.

But as we will learn later, hearing from God is not completely up to us. God will communicate His will to a believer using the medium best suited for the maturity level of that believer. It is God who opens our ear, and He is the one who teaches us His voice. So Jesus can assuredly say, *"My sheep hear My voice... and they follow Me"* *(John 10:27)*

The *Letter* Versus the *Spirit* of the Word

Let me address an issue we touched on in an earlier chapter that may at first appear to be controversial but is not, when considered in proper light. It is not the *letter* of the words printed in the Bible that is the word of God but the *spirit* of those words. This is the reason we can have so many versions of the Bible, each translating particular verses or passages differently, and yet maintaining the truth of God intact.

In fact, there are a few words and texts in the Bible whose underlying original Hebrew words are still unclear to modern translators. But in spite of our imperfect knowledge of those texts, we can still know the will of God He is communicating to us.

First Corinthians 3:6 should enlighten us: *"...the letter kills, but the spirit gives life."* Throughout history, groups of people, claiming justification from particular Scriptures in the Bible, have committed horrific atrocities against other groups. Wars, racism, hatred and even murders have been perpetrated in the name of God, based on the distorted interpretation of the *letter* of the Bible.

Therefore, when it comes to interpreting Scriptures, we should exercise great care and heed Jesus' advice in John 6:63: *"It is the spirit that gives life, the flesh profits nothing. The words that I speak to you are spirit and they are life."* We cannot approach the Scriptures primarily from an intellectual perspective. If natural intelligence was a spiritual asset, then only the best minds could receive the deeper truths of Scriptures.

On the contrary, it is the Holy Spirit that imparts understanding of the Scriptures to us. Jesus said it was the Holy Spirit who would lead us into all truth; and He does this by leading us through our regenerated spirit. Studying the Bible daily without the guidance of the Holy Spirit will get us nowhere closer to the truth than where we started. Paul writes in 2 Timothy 3:7 about some people *"always learning and never able to come to the knowledge of the truth."*

Personally, I believe that God designed the *letter* of the Scriptures to be fluid, and open to diverse interpretation on purpose. The basis for this belief lies in the typology of the *'flaming sword that turned every way'* mentioned in Genesis 3:24. God placed this sword at the east of the Garden of Eden to guard the way to the Tree of Life. In a similar fashion and purpose, the Scriptures, as the sword of the spirit, also *turn every way,* with the potential to say what they were not meant to say.

How does this fluidity serve God's purpose? The same reason God gave for placing the flaming sword in the Garden of Eden: so Adam and Eve would not eat of the Tree of Life and live forever in their fallen state. Just as the flaming sword that turned every way guarded the way to the Tree of Life, the fluidity of the Bible serves to guard the way to eternal life.

The Bible is very clear: Jesus is the only name given by God to save man (Acts 4:12). And we know from 1 Peter 1:23 that the new birth of the believer happens through the word of God.

Accordingly, the flexibility of the scriptures ensures that no one without faith in the Lord Jesus can taste eternal life and live forever in their unregenerate condition. Said in a different way, it is only the truth revealed by the Holy Spirit that has the capacity to impart life to an unregenerate man. This is how we are born of the Spirit (see John 3). Therefore, understanding of the scriptures that is only the result of an intellectual appraisal is totally useless in the spiritual birth experience.

There are certain truths in the Bible that no stretch of intellectual prowess can touch. Only God can take us there, as we are about to learn later. In fact, Paul states emphatically in 1 Corinthians 2:14 that the natural man cannot receive the things of God because they are spiritually discerned. So, when Jesus said in John 6:63 that the words he spoke were spirit and life, it should be sufficient proof that the natural intellect of man is completely useless in apprehending spiritual truths.

It is true that some people without the Holy Spirit are still able to preach the Bible with all eloquence and fervency. But the question is, do they impart anything of spiritual value to their hearers? All they can accomplish is a good motivational speech that moves the emotions of their hearers, but does absolutely nothing to affect their spiritual state.

Spiritual Guidance versus Spiritual Hearing

Now, there is also a spiritual guidance that is different from hearing the voice of God. We have already defined hearing as knowledge or understanding we receive in our spirit. Guidance from the Holy Spirit, however, is not always *audible*, or a reception of a particular understanding or knowledge.

In Psalm 32, which we discussed in chapter 7, we learned that God was not going to speak to us at every moment in our lives as what we need to accomplish. But He speaks of guiding us with His Eye. We interpreted the *Eye* of God to be the Holy Spirit. In my own experience, this guidance comes in a form where we sense: *restraints* from taking an action; or a *burden* to undertake a particular action; or a feeling of *excitement* in our spirit, confirming a breakthrough; or a flood of *peace* in our heart, suggesting approval or an answer. These are impressions left in our spirit by the Holy Spirit, as He guides us along the paths or life.

The intuition that is of our soul is subtly different from this guidance in our spirit. The hunches and gut-feelings we may receive from our natural intuition are not as accurate as the spiritual guidance we receive from the Holy Spirit. Those who have experienced spiritual guidance of the Holy Spirit know with certainty whether the Holy Spirit wants them to take or not to take a particular action in a matter. Natural intuition, on the other hand, is not so definite, and may or may not happen as felt. Moreover, the efficacy of natural intuition is entirely dependent on the predisposition of the person receiving it.

For instance, a person, who by nature or nurture is a risk-taker, may act quickly on a gut feeling not because his intuition is any more definite, but because such a person is not afraid to take risks. If the person's intellectual appraisal of the matter agrees with his intuition, then he will be moved to take action. In contrast, a person who is moved by the Holy Spirit has a definite sense of action, even though his intellect might disagree.

In fact, spiritual intuition, for the most part, transcends common sense. It might take several years to discover the logic behind why God wanted us to take certain actions during a particular time in our lives. The following story from my own experience demonstrates that what we hear from God may not always coincide with common sense. The story also shows that, if God spoke to you, the results would always bear it out.

In 1987, I received admission to a graduate school in the United States. I lived in Ghana at that time. The problem was that I did not receive any financial aid or assistantship from the school. But without any form of financial assistance, it was virtually impossible to pay for my college in the United States. It would have required me saving my gross salaries for a number of years to be able to afford the required tuition for just one year in graduate school. And believe me, at the time, I had a well-paid job by the economic standards of a developing nation.

A second problem was that I had not yet obtained a visa to be able travel to the United States. And back in those days of political and economic instability in my country, seeking to travel to the United States was like seeking to enter a fortress, so to speak. Only about ten percent of visa applicants could enter the US consulate office on any given day. And of those who succeeded, only a few actually got a travel visa to the United States. The rest of the applicants were either turned down outright, or given a laundry list of near-impossible conditions to fulfill before the consular would consider even their application for a visa.

Faced with this scenario, I decided to do the most logical thing first: I needed to secure financial assistance before thinking about a travel visa. Because of the time involved to apply for an assistantship, I asked the graduate school to defer my admission to the following spring semester, hoping to get an assistantship by that time. I calculated that it would take more than six months before I could possibly travel to the United States. Knowing the significant hurdles I needed to overcome in order to fulfill my dream of a graduate school in the United States, I engaged a trusted friend to help me pray for divine intervention—I needed a miracle!

This was where the Holy Spirit stepped in. No, I did not get a miracle right then. One day, while I was praying with my friend, the Holy Spirit said, "resign from your job immediately." Well, that was not what I had expected to hear. This was not the first time I was hearing the voice of the Holy Spirit in my spirit. So I knew God was speaking to me; but nothing in that directive made any sense to me at the time. My friend, who I considered more spiritually matured than I was, worsened my discomfort when he asked me if I was sure I had heard from God. Now, I was no longer sure, not because I did not believe I had heard from God, but because of the enormous sacrifice required to obey that directive.

Did I mention my country was facing both political and economic instability at the time? Well, the unemployment rate was well over thirty-five percent during those years, and just having a job was an enormous blessing. Besides, the job I had at the time was one of the most lucrative jobs any young man fresh out of college could wish for. So giving up that job on just a whim was quirky, to say the least.

But the mother of all insensibility: I still had nearly six months to wait before I could confirm whether or not I would get the financial assistance or the indomitable United States visa. Nothing made any sense at all in the directive to quit my job immediately.

I know some people have God all figured out, wrapped up and placed in a box, and cannot see how such a directive could possibly have come from God. I know about God's indictment against people who would not work (see 2 Thessalonians 3:10). In fact, I considered that Scripture in evaluating what I had heard from the Holy Spirit. But Paul in that Scripture was referring to persons who were disorderly, busybodies and refused to work due to their laziness. Okay, let me finish my testimony so you can judge more accurately for yourself.

I prayed: "Lord, if this is truly you, send me an encouragement to quit my job." The encouragement came the very next day. It was a Sunday. A businesswoman I knew approached me: "Can you spare two weeks to help me get this once-in-a-lifetime deal through." I told her that I was just planning to quit my job. She was elated: "Excellent, get that done, and come and see me immediately! We have very little time."

Those of you who have never lived in a developing nation with a serious economic crisis may have a hard time understanding the importance of such news. But that was all the encouragement I needed from God. It was a perfect situation. That mega business deal could bring instant wealth, if all went well.

Did I say I trusted this business friend? Well, I did, and proceeded to resign from my job the very next day. I knew no one would understand my decision, so I resigned from the job before sharing the *good* news with my parents and close friends. Needless to say, my parents were furious, and my friends were shocked. Everybody else that heard of my decision thought I had lost a few screws in my brain. I thought so too after the reality of my action began to set in.

To make a long story short, that business deal never materialized due to one disappointment or another, none the businesswoman's fault. Did I not ask the Lord to send me an *encouragement* to quit my job? That was all there was to the mega business deal. God sent the businesswoman to help me make that faith jump.

However, God had a different plan to sustain me through this season of no job. He arranged a miraculous provision that gave me more income than I was earning when I had a job. This miracle was so phenomenal that I was still getting paid two years after I had left the country, and had accomplished all my other goals.

Talking about goals, I did get the assistantship from the graduate school; and I did get a visa to study in the United States through another miraculous intervention from God. But most importantly, the reason God wanted me to quit my job at the time he asked me would became apparent when I came to the United States, and faced some of the toughest trials I had ever faced in my Christian life.

God used those six months of unemployment to prepare me in ways that would not have been possible if I had been burdened with a full time job. The Holy Spirit took me into depths of prayer I had never experienced before. Also, I learned so much about God, and became more intimate with Him during that time. I matured in so many ways in the spirit, and best of all, I learned to hear the voice of God more clearly. The seeds for most of the things I am writing in this book were birthed in me during those times.

So I did hear from God at the time, even though what I heard appeared to violate all common sense. With time, common sense caught up with God's wisdom. But what a tragic loss of spiritual effectiveness that would have resulted, if I had been guided only by common sense! I bear witness that the word of God will accomplish the purpose for which it was sent. If we truly hear from God, and obey by faith, that same word is able to sustain us through any need, want, or care.

There is enough goofiness in the name of God among Christians such that a testimony like this runs the risk of being misinterpreted by someone without understanding. Therefore, I sense a need to caution that this testimony in no way disparages common sense in everyday living, or encourages recklessness and irresponsible actions—all in the name of hearing from God. My story was about a unique dealing by God regarding a unique person in a unique situation, and should be viewed in that context accordingly.

As 2 Thessalonians 3:10 shows, God is not pleased with busy-bodies and lazy believers. In my situation, because it was God who spoke to me, He also ensured that I had no financial struggles for obeying His voice to quit my job. In fact, I had abundance and an overflow of financial blessing that continued for two years after I had left for the United States. This result proved I had truly heard from God.

We should also be aware that hearing from God does not necessarily exempt us from hardships in carrying out God's will. In fact, for the most part we face persecution *because* of the word we hear, as Jesus revealed in The Parable of the Sower (Mark 4:3-20). During the six months that I have described above, I experienced plenty of trials, uncertainties and fears, while God taught me how to trust Him regardless of any circumstances.

How Do We Hear in the Spirit?

> *"He awakens my ear* to hear as the learned. The *Lord God has opened my ear*; and I was not rebellious…"* (Isaiah 50:4-5—emphasis added)

> "Sacrifice and offering You did not desire, *my ear you have opened…"* (Psalm 40:6—emphasis added)

The above Scriptures plainly reveal that hearing the voice of God is not completely up to us. It is God who opens our ears to hear, as both scriptures say. This is why you cannot miss hearing the voice of God once you become acquainted with His voice.

We previously stated that spiritual hearing is not a physical activity. God opens our ears by, as Paul describes it in Ephesians 1:18, *"…the eyes of your understanding being enlightened."* God makes us understand what He is saying to us by whatever means. God is not restricted in the media He uses to speak to us.

Even though hearing in the spirit is not necessarily an auditory phenomenon, God does speak audibly to people sometimes. Generally, however, spiritual hearing is about receiving insight or understanding in the spirit regarding a matter. Thus, when we receive information that opens our understanding to what God wants, we just heard from the Spirit of God, irrespective of the media He used.

In Matthew 16:17, when Peter recognized who Jesus was, Jesus said that it was the Father who had revealed that knowledge to Him. Jesus through the spirit was able to recognize that what Peter said did not come to him through a mere intellectual appraisal of what Jesus had been doing till that point in time. Peter's understanding had the stamp of the Spirit of God on it.

The reason we can say this is because, in John 1:49, Nathanael also recognized Jesus was the Son of God after Jesus had told him he saw him under the fig tree. But Nathanael's insight was due to an intellectual enlightenment, which was the result of him seeing Jesus perform a miracle. That is why Jesus responded: *"Do you believe all this just because I told you I had seen you under the fig tree"* (John 1:50—NLT)? Both Nathanael and Peter recognized Jesus as the Son of God; but only Peter's information was affirmed as coming from God.

Remember what we learned earlier? In the spirit world, it is the spirit of the words we use that is received, not the mere letter of the words we use. If God does not open our ears to hear, then what we hear is the result of our own reasoning or an interjection by the enemy.

We noted in Chapter 7 that God has already spoken, or is yet speaking; and it takes earthly time for man to catch up to what He has said. According to Psalm 119:89, God's word is already settled in Heaven. And by the Lord's Prayer (Matthew 6:10), we understand that God's heart is for His will to be done on earth, as it is done in heaven.

To realize that goal, God opens our ears to hear His word for a particular purpose that needs to be established in the earth at a particular time. When we hear the word of God, it might appear that God just started speaking to us. What actually happened was that God enlightened our understanding to what He has already settled in Heaven.

Also in talking about man's dominion in the earth, we showed that man could achieve full dominion only through the knowledge of God. It is the process of acquiring this knowledge that would transform man into the likeness of God, by which man would have the unlimited capacity to take full dominion.

It is this process that makes time necessary on earth. Even though we discovered that time is an illusion, God placed man in time on purpose. Time was instituted to enable man to order priorities, and measure progress, as he plans and executes to attain dominion in the earth. (There is more to this subject, but we are unable to fully discuss it here as it is beyond the scope of this book.)

The fact is, when man reaches the appropriate stage of spiritual growth or maturity, God opens his ears (unlocks his understanding), so he can hear a particular word to set his course for the next stage in the process. What process? The process of becoming like God or, more directly, like the Son of God. This is God's goal for every believer and, for that matter, the Church, as stated in Ephesians 4:13: *"...Till we all come to the unity of the faith and of the knowledge of the Son of God, to a perfect man, to the measure of the stature of the fullness of Christ."*

Maturity is required in spiritual hearing, because of the worth and power of God's word. Maturity levels are attained through the choices we make. That means we can grow as fast or as slow as we want, depending how much we cooperate with the Holy Spirit.

We spent three chapters in this book to demonstrate that the word that proceeds out of the mouth of God is the most precious thing in the entire universe. And because it is the true riches, God does not dispense it indiscriminately. Jesus instructed us in Matthew 7:6 not to give what is holy to a dog, and not to cast our pearls before the swine. Therefore, I could not imagine Him casting His precious word before those who would trample on it.

After we enter into the kingdom of God, we come to discover that possessing anything in God's kingdom is based on qualification; and qualification is measured in faithfulness and maturity. This is actually designed to be so for our own good, for reasons we have already mentioned.

Additionally, the Bible says that the word of God is sharper than a double-edged sword (Hebrews 4:12). And no responsible parent would put anything that is sharper than a double-edged sword in the hands of an immature child.

The same word of God can become a blessing or a curse, depending on how it is received. This is the message of Deuteronomy 28. Curses and blessings are the two sides of the same coin; which side we get depends on what response we give to the word of God that comes to us.

According to Hebrews 2:2, the word of God that came through angels carried the full extent of God's authority, such that every violation or disobedience of that word was punished. How then can we escape punishment, if we mishandle the word of God that comes through Christ (Hebrew 1:2)? This is one of the reasons God does not speak directly to everybody indiscriminately, but mostly to those who have the maturity to handle it properly.

The Problem With Not Growing into Maturity

The key to receiving victories in certain areas of our lives is in hearing a specific word of God in each of those areas. Yet we are learning that God will open our ear to hear His word based on our spiritual maturity level (more about this later).

This is where a lot of Christians encounter frustrations. They hear the wonderful promises of God and desire them with all their heart, but they are unwilling to go through the process of growth that will qualify them for those blessings.

Now understand this: God's blessings are for every one of His children. He is no respecter of persons. Nevertheless, God's blessings are not accessible to us indiscriminately. Some of God's blessings are available to us just because we are born again. Others are available to us just because someone prayed or interceded for us. But there are some blessings that are available to us only because we qualify for them.

There are keys to different levels of authority in the kingdom of God; and these keys are available to only those who qualify. No amount of prayer, worship, praise, or all the other religious duties Christians perform can get us into those blessings, if we do not qualify.

Listen to Paul's reason for not being able to feed the Corinthian church certain truths:

> Dear brothers and sisters, when I was with you I couldn't talk to you as I would to mature Christians. I had to talk as though you belonged to this world or as though you were infants in the Christian life. I had to feed you with milk and not with solid food, **because you couldn't handle anything stronger.** And you still aren't ready, for you are still controlled by your own sinful desires (1 Corinthians 3:1-3 – NLT)

And here is what Galatians 4:1 also says about immaturity:

Now I say that the heir, as long as he is a child, does not differ at all from a slave, though he is master of all, but is under guardians and stewards until the time appointed by the father.

The immature Christian has little or no spiritual fruit that would differentiate him from an unbeliever. Hence, he is also unqualified to handle deeper revelations from the Holy Spirit. He is only able to receive milk, because he is a babe. And as we learned in Hebrew 5:13, whoever uses milk is unskillful in the word of righteousness. But Hebrew 1:9 reveals that the scepter (the symbol of authority) of God's kingdom is a scepter of righteousness. Therefore the immature believer cannot rule in life, because he is unskillful in the word of righteousness.

The point is, although Christ has bequeathed to us, as children of God, an inheritance of unimaginable wealth, our immaturity prevents us from accessing most of it presently. Notice in Galatians 4:1 quoted above, that the status of the child changes at the *"time appointed by the Father"*. God is the one that determines when we are ready to receive a particular truth. Therefore, it is God who opens our ear to hear, as we have established.

Even so, we are still responsible for how fast we mature as Christians. Let me say this again at the risk of overemphasis: Self-determination, which equates to freedom of choice, is the greatest privilege God gave man; and how we exercise this privilege is the difference between living under a blessing or living under a curse.

It is because of self-determination that each one of us must diligently work out his or her own salvation. It is because of self-determination that we have to acknowledge God for Him to step into our world. It is because of self-determination that prayer is necessary. And it is because of self-determination that the kingdom of God allows people who are determined (violent) to seize it by force.

This is why we have to pursue God on purpose to apprehend Him; this is why salvation is for whosoever wills; this is why faith is a deliberate, willful choice to trust God at His word. And this is why the subject of Chapter 10—the Law of Reciprocity—is very important.

To sum up what we have learned so far, we emphasize that we have to hear from God in order to achieve dominion in the earth. As we have demonstrated over and again, the word of God is His very essence; therefore, when God speaks to us, He is revealing His nature to us. And according to 1 Peter 1:5, we are able to share in God's divine nature through the knowledge He imparts to us. It is this transformation into the likeness of God that empowers us to attain dominion in the earth.

Yet due to the principle of self-determination, we have to purposefully pursue God in order to hear from Him and to receive knowledge from His mouth. In the Bible, the people of God had to *consecrate* themselves to engage the presence of God. In the Old Testament, for instance, this consecration was an elaborate procedure that called for the full attention of the person being consecrated. This was God's way of telling His children that, in order for Him to get involved in their affairs, they have to choose to have Him involved.

The truth is, everything in the kingdom of God is constituted to work in this manner. Freedom of choice affirms man's sovereignty over his destiny, and God will not violate this sovereignty, even if man continues to choose wrongly. We demonstrate our faith in God when we deny ourselves the freedom to pursue our own ambitions, and choose to pursue God's will. And the more freedom we submit to God, the more of His kingdom and its power become accessible to us. In yielding our freedom to God, we are robbing ourselves of our own ambitions in exchange for more of God's kingdom. This, in essence, is *spiritual violence*, which we discuss more broadly in the next chapter.

God's Media of Communication

God does speak—sometimes one way and sometimes another. He speaks even though men may not understand it. God may speak in a dream or a vision of the night. This is when men are in a deep sleep and lying in their beds. He may speak in their ears... (Job 33:14-16a - NLT).

The basic message of the above quotation from Job 33 is two-fold: that God speaks to man; and that God uses different media to communicate with man. God is not restricted in the media He uses to communicate His will to man. The only thing that restricts what God will do or not do is His own word, but Psalm 119:96 says His word has no limits.

I have heard some people say that God only speaks in a still small voice, basing their argument on 1 King 19:12, where the voice of God came to Elijah softly. But if we read that passage carefully, we discover that God speaking in a *still small voice*—in a *soft whisper* (as other translations put it)—was a relatively newer experience for Elijah.

Apparently, Elijah was accustomed to some level of fanfare whenever God spoke to him. No doubt, Elijah would have read about God speaking to the children of Israel on Mount Horeb, where God spoke with such drama that no one could endure the sight (see full reference below). And Elijah's own experience included God answering his prayer with fire from heaven (see 1 Kings 18:24).

Thus, in 1 Kings 19:12, when Elijah was witnessing another earth-shattering drama, he logically expected God to speak in the midst of that familiar fanfare. This is the reason for the recurring phrase in that scripture: *"but the LORD was not in the"* wind or earthquake. The word *'but'* suggests an outcome different from what Elijah expected. Thus, we conclude that the *'still small voice'* was either unexpected or relatively new to Elijah

We needed to clarify this matter, because every time we confine God to a set of rules based on incomplete revelation, we deprive a lot of God's children from accessing particular blessings of the kingdom of God. The truth is, throughout the Scriptures, God spoke to His people using different media as it pleased Him.

In the Old Testament, for instance, God spoke to His people through: an audible voice, angelic visitations, dreams, visions, prophets, and the written word. God also spoke to people using ordinary people, circumstances, miracles, inanimate objects, and even animals.

Incidentally, we can identify some of the same media of communication God used in the Old Testament also in the New Testament. All of this goes to underscore what we revealed about the reality in the spirit realm earlier: In the spirit, it is not the mode, media or method of transaction that counts; it is rather the essence of what is being exchanged that counts.

So let us learn this again: when God makes us understand His will by whatever means, He just spoke to us, and we just heard from God! And we repeat Job 33:14 for fresh enlightenment: *"God does speak—sometimes one way and sometimes another. He speaks even though men may not understand it."* So God has spoken, or is yet speaking, using different media of communication. But the question is, do we have the ear to hear what He is saying to us?

The communication media used by God throughout the Bible, as listed above, are not meant to be exhaustive. What is worth noting though is that not much changed between the Old and the New Testaments in the way God spoke to His people. But the manner of operation of some of these media in the Old Testament may be different from the one used in the New Testament.

For instance, in the Old Testament, God did speak with audible voice to His people at one time or the other. In fact, in Exodus 19, God spoke to the whole nation of Israel from Mount Horeb, and it was not a pretty sight when He did. According to Hebrews 12:21, *"so terrifying was the sight that Moses said, 'I am exceedingly afraid and trembling'."*

We understand that God did speak to them in that frightening way because He wanted them to have utmost respect for His word no matter how it was delivered. Also, since Moses was God's main prophet to the people, He wanted Israel to accord the same respect for His word through Moses, as they would respect the word directly out of God's mouth.

When we come to the New Testament, God spoke audibly to Peter, John and James during the transfiguration of Jesus on the mountain. Also when Jesus was baptized in the Jordan River, God spoke audibly to affirm His Son. Even here it is not so obvious whether everyone around heard the message, or whether only Jesus heard it. The Book of Acts of the Apostles also documents several instances of God and angels speaking directly to the apostles and other believers. So even though God is speaking audibly to people in both the Old and the New Testaments, the intensity of speaking is markedly different between the two periods.

Real as these examples of God speaking audibly to people is, they also show the scant direct evidence in the Bible for God to communicate with man in this manner. In other words, we can cite only a few recorded instances when God spoke directly to man. Even, when we see God talking to Noah or Abraham, for instance, we should also be aware that these men would not hear from God for long periods of time before He spoke to them again.

The Scriptures:
God's Basic Media of Communication with Man

When we stated previously that the letter of the Bible, by itself, is not the powerful word of God, some readers may have misunderstood what that blunt statement meant. But the truth is, God does speak to us primarily through the Scriptures. In fact, the Scriptures are the most objective source of God's will for man on earth today.

However, the *letter* of the word is merely the vehicle God uses to communicate His will to man, but it does not equate to the *spirit* of the word itself. As explained before, the letter of the Scriptures can be interpreted to mean all sorts of things without touching the truth of God. Even so, God speaks to us directly out of the Scriptures.

Yet in spite of the completeness of Scriptures as we have it today, man is still the principal agent and, therefore, the mouthpiece of God in the earth for all time. God used men and women to communicate or interpret His will in the Old Testament, and He is still using men and women to do the same today. Any doctrine that devalues the role of man as the mouthpiece of God to only a historical context is not from God.

The ministry gifts Christ gave to the church, as mentioned in Ephesians 4, are God's preferred way to equip His people for the establishment of His kingdom in the earth today. It amazes me how some people can vehemently deny the legitimacy of both apostles and prophets in our time, and embrace teachers and pastors, even though they are all mentioned in the same verse of Scripture as having something to do with edifying the body of Christ for ministry work (see 1 Corinthians 12:28 and Ephesians 4:11).

Men and women called and sent by God carry His word, and we would do a lot better if we paid attention to their message. This is where the authority of Scriptures is most needed to confirm whether what we hear is of God or of the flesh. Nevertheless, if we marginalize the men and women of God given to the body of Christ, we stand in danger of marginalizing the word of God through them.

I personally can testify that because I have some measure of understanding in this area, I give utmost respect to the men and women who preach God's word. In doing so, God has rewarded my faith greatly by sending many answers I needed through them. Sometimes, I receive answers to specific questions through anointed preachers on the very next day after I have asked God those questions.

It is not that these men and women of God are more righteous than other children of God. Nor can we assume that because a person is being used of God, he or she is, necessarily, stronger or more matured than others not so used. Rather, these ministers of God are equipped with unique gifts and special grace (see Ephesians 4:7)) to nurture the people of God for particular usefulness in the kingdom of God.

Therefore, when we are planted under an anointed minister of God, we can get to our spiritual destination faster than we can do all by ourselves. Of the myriads of promises in the Bible, which one is relevant to us now in our journey with God? Or, of the countless purposes we can accomplish for God in the world, which ones are we best suited to fulfill at this present time in our lives? That we cannot easily find trusted answers to these questions is the reason for Ephesians 4:11-13:

> And He Himself gave some to be apostles, some
> prophets, some evangelists, and some pastors and
> teachers, for the equipping of the saints for the work

of ministry, for the edifying of the body of Christ, till we all come to the unity of the faith and of the knowledge of the Son of God, to a perfect man, to the measure of the stature of the fullness of Christ...

Therefore the question is not whether apostles and prophets are for our times, but whether those who profess to be apostles and prophets are truly gifted by Christ for those offices.

Spiritual Hearing Is Accomplished Only Through Our Human Spirit

Irrespective of what medium God uses to communicate with us today, He imparts truth to us in our regenerated human spirit. Our human spirit is the temple of the Holy Ghost. That is where communion takes place; that is where fellowship takes place; and that is where true worship takes place. According to John 4:24, God is Spirit, and those who worship Him *must* worship Him *in spirit* and in truth. Therefore, let every believer know that in all things pertaining to God, our natural faculties play only a secondary role and never a leading role.

The reason we cannot trust our natural faculties, especially our human intellect, in spiritual things is that our Adamic nature is trained to function after the pattern of the world system—a system of which Satan is the god. And as we came to know, this old nature is not only completely useless in the things of the spirit, it actually resists the things of God. Romans 8:7 says that the carnal mind is enmity against God, and cannot be subject to the law of God.

I know some sincere believers are trying very hard to recondition their old nature to conform to the things of God. But I can also testify of how hopelessly frustrating that is. Those who persist in serving God with their carnal mind run the risk of shipwrecking their faith. This is what Paul realized in Roman 7:18, in regard to the flesh: *"For I know that in me (that is, in my flesh) nothing good dwells."* And here was his cry of desperation after he realized the hopelessness of trying to fix his old nature: *"O wretched man that I am! Who will deliver me from this body of death?"*

Because of this weakness in our flesh, the only way our natural intellect will become useful in the things of the spirit is for it to be re-trained after the pattern of God's system. This is a renewal the Holy Spirit accomplishes in us over time, as he teaches us the knowledge of God. Over time, part of our maturity is a renewed mind that allows us to be able to discern between good and evil according to God's standards.

Even at this stage of maturity, our renewed mind does not usurp the leading role of our regenerated spirit. The renewed mind simply becomes a powerful agent of our spirit man to establish the will of God in the earth. Instead of resisting the will of God, our renewed mind now cooperates with it, harmonizing with the mind of Christ in us.

CHAPTER 9

PURSUING TO HEAR FROM GOD

Again, the kingdom of Heaven is like treasure hidden in a field, which a man found and hid; and for joy over it he goes and sells all that he has and buys that field. Again, the kingdom of Heaven is like a merchant seeking beautiful pearls, who, when he had found one pearl of great price, went and sold all that he had and bought it (Matthew 13: 44-46).

Violence in the Spirit: Taking the Kingdom by Force

The kingdom of God is about God's character, power and authority. It is not a physical entity but a mindset. Hence it is not recognizable by simple observation. This is what Jesus meant by *"the kingdom of God does not come with observation"* (Luke 17:20). To inherit the kingdom of God is a journey of being transformed into the God's likeness—His way of thinking and doing things. This transformation is accomplished through the knowledge of God. And this knowledge is acquired through the word that comes out of God's mouth.

When we recognize the value of knowing God, and place it at the highest pinnacle in our lives, then God's kingdom and its power become accessible to us. That is why Jesus said we must seek first the kingdom of God and its righteousness, and then all other things would be added unto us (Matthew 6:33).

We attribute worth to anything by the amount of time and effort we spend on that thing. Time and effort can be measured in money, because money is compressed time and effort. In other words, Money represents the time and effort that went into the creation, development and production of an idea. That is how money becomes a measure of worth (or the price of a thing); therefore the price we are willing to pay for an item indicates how much worth we place on that item.

In Matthew 13:44-46 quoted above, Jesus signifies the price required to inherit the full rights to the kingdom of God. This price also defines the *violence*, which Jesus indicated in Matthew 11:12 was necessary to possess the kingdom of God. Giving up everything in life to follow God is robbing everything else of its time and priority in our lives to give to the pursuit of God.

Note that, in Matthew 13:44-46, the persons involved sold *everything* to purchase the one thing dearest to them. The word *everything* should be taken literally, because whatever we withhold from God will become our loss in the kingdom of God, according to another spiritual law that we will discuss in Chapter 10.

But someone may wonder if God really requires us to sacrifice *everything* we hold dear to our hearts in order to possess His kingdom. Jesus does not leave the answer to this question to our imagination or personal preference:

> Whoever desires to come after Me, let him deny himself, and take up his cross, and follow Me. For whoever desires to save his life will lose it, but whoever loses his life for My sake and the gospel's will save it (Mark 8:34, 35).

Therefore, my unequivocal answer to that same question is: yes, God really requires us to sacrifice everything to have full access to

His kingdom! To even wonder about that question shows that we lack revelation of who God is and what His kingdom represents to us. The truth is, there is nothing we hold dear in our present life that compares to the glory of what we can possess when we give up everything for the sake of God's kingdom.

The mixed blessings we experience in our lives today are the direct results of not giving up everything to pursue God's kingdom. And the reason we hold back parts of our lives from God is because our trust in Him is not complete.

Ignorance is at the root of this incomplete trust. And this same lack of understanding is why people in Jesus' day found His message too impractical to follow. Jesus said some seemingly hard things to reveal God's standards for man to possess His kingdom, and to have complete fellowship with Him. Here are two classic ones:

> If any man come to me, and hate not his father, and mother, and wife, and children, and brethren, and sisters, yea, and his own life also, he cannot be my disciple (Luke 14:26).

> And every one that hath forsaken houses, or brethren, or sisters, or father, or mother, or wife, or children, or lands, for my name's sake, shall receive an hundred-fold, and shall inherit everlasting life (Matthew 9:29).

Anyone who did anything of eternal value for God had to leave all. Abraham left all; Moses left all; and Paul left all. The disciples of Jesus left all: *"Then Peter said to him, 'we've given up everything to follow you. What will we get out of it'"* (Matthew 9:27)?

However, giving up everything for the sake of God's kingdom should not be an occasion of grief for us. We must get the revelation Paul received, and be grateful God chose to reveal the same truth to us. Listen to Paul's reaction when he discovered the truth of giving up everything for the sake of Christ:

> I once thought all these things were so very important, but now I consider them worthless because of what

> Christ has done. Yes, everything else is worthless
> when compared with the priceless gain of knowing
> Christ Jesus my Lord. I have discarded every-
> thing else, counting it all as garbage, so that I may
> have Christ and become one with him (Philippians
> 3:7-9—NLT).

Yes, everything else we hold dear presently will pale in value compared to what Christ will reveal in us when we completely become His. This is not a loss but an immeasurable gain.

I know that we live on planet earth, and we have a lot of natural desires and needs. In fact, God created us natural beings on purpose, and He incorporated all the desires of our souls in us on purpose. He actually promises to fulfill our heart desires, if we delight ourselves in Him (Psalm 37:4). But the issue here is not about things, wants or needs; it is about priorities, affections and love. *"Seek...first the kingdom...and all these **things will be added"** is the issue at stake here.

Also, we should clarify that denying ourselves is not about subjecting our lives under harsh conditions to gain some measure of righteousness, holiness or a state of perfection. Rather, it is about choosing to let go our personal ambitions to pursue God's purpose for us. It is about pursuing God's appointed destiny to the denial of where our own interests and natural talents would take us. It is also about consistently choosing God's will over anything, when that thing—family, business or pleasure—is in conflict with His will.

Therefore, in denying ourselves, God's will becomes the standard by which we prioritize everything in our lives. Everything is judged in the light of God's will, and anything that is in conflict with it is rejected.

So pursuing God is recognizing who God is, ascribing to Him the worth due Him, and giving up everything to be acquainted with Him. This is the highest ideal of faith, which pleases God so much that Hebrews 11:6 says He rewards those who pursue Him with that level of diligence. We will talk about the rewards later, but it suffices to say that there are tremendous rewards in serving the Lord with our whole heart.

Hence, when we become too busy to give our full attention to the will of God, it is because we do not believe God has a better deal than whatever we are currently pursuing on our own. Such a belief is obviously a lie—the same lie Satan told Adam and Eve. Satan proposed to them an alternative that seemed to be a better deal than what God had told them.

This was the same lie the children of Israel believed, when they desired to return to Egypt rather than follow the vision God had chosen for them. But we know, according to Deuteronomy 5:29, that God's vision for the Israelites was entirely for their benefit:

> Oh, that they would always have hearts like this, that they might fear me and obey all my commands! If they did, they and their descendants would prosper forever—NLT.

Today, God wants us also to have the same level of reverence for His word, as He required of the Israelites in their journey with Him. We should be able to give up everything to pursue God's word, if we understand that we cannot achieve anything of eternal value without God's word. And giving up everything to pursue the word of God is *spiritual violence*, which we describe below.

Elements of Spiritual Violence:
The Persistence of Faith

When Jesus said in Matthew 11:22 that the kingdom of heaven allows violence, and the violent takes it by force, he was talking about the *attitude* of those who have the understanding of the kingdom of God, and the faith to possess its power here in this life. The Bible teaches that the kingdom of God is already here, and it is in us (Luke 17:20). Yet it is also true that the full manifestation of the influence of God's kingdom is in a future setting.

This is indeed the nature of most of God's promises. Because God lives outside of time, and is not subject to time limitations, He sees every promise He makes as already accomplished. God calls things that are not as though they were; and He declares the end from the beginning (see Romans 4:17 and Isaiah 46:10).

But we learned in Chapter 7 that time is an illusionary phenomenon established by God to accomplish certain things in man, as man journeys through eternity. We also learned that, by faith, we too could transcend the limitations of time and benefit from things that are present with God now, but are not yet manifested in the physical realm.

This was how Mary was able to compel Jesus to perform a miracle, even though it was not yet time for Jesus to reveal himself (John 2:1-11). Mary's aggression in her faith overrode Jesus' reluctance to step outside of his time. Therefore, by that act of spiritual violence, Mary took the kingdom of God by force!

The Syrophenecian woman in Mark 7:28 also took the kingdom of God by force. Jesus had declared in Matthew 15-24 that He was sent to the lost sheep of Israel, and here, in Mark 7:28, was this woman without a covenant with God, seeking for her child healing, which was meant for the children of God. But by the persistence of faith, she was able to seize that kingdom benefit for her child. We know that God was going to bring the gentiles into His family through the sacrificial death of Jesus in a future period. Yet that did not stop God from releasing a blessing to that gentile woman outside of the ordained time.

Intensity of Desire

Through the intensity of desire, Elisha was able to obtain a double portion anointing from Elijah (2 Kings 2:9-12). Elisha was already chosen by God to replace Elijah; and Elisha would have, ordinarily, carried the usual anointing of a prophet. But Elisha did not give up everything he had—his career, family and birthright— just to become an ordinary prophet! He certainly did not want to start from scratch, building his own ministry, as did his master Elijah. He rather wanted to start from where Elijah finished, standing on his master's shoulders, to reach for more of God's kingdom.

Elisha's desire for this double-portion blessing was so intense that nothing could dissuade him from following Elijah all the way to possess the blessing. And not even the powerful whirlwind that took his master away could distract Elisha from receiving his heart desire.

Similarly, Jacob received the blessing to be the progenitor of a mighty nation by an aggressive pursuit that culminated in wrestling all night with God for the promise. Jacob had always desired this promise even before his birth, challenging his twin-brother in the womb for the birthright to it, tricking his brother for the right to it, deceiving his father for the blessing to it. And, in Genesis 32, we see him wrestling with God for the key to it. Jacob did not let go until he prevailed and obtained his blessing. Nature, tradition and human weakness were staggering barriers to Jacob's dream; but his passion for the dream was stronger than all of them.

We do not have sufficient time to describe the boldness of faith, wherein David, Daniel, Shadrach, Meshach and Abed-Nego distinguished themselves, and accessed the power of God's kingdom. All of their stories suggest one thing: that faith is an aggressive stance in the spirit.

And describing this stance as violent is appropriate because it is essentially the clash of two dimensions—the visible versus the invisible. It is superimposing spiritual laws over natural laws. It is also a clash of kingdoms: the kingdom of light against the kingdom of darkness.

To be able to take such an aggressive stance in the spirit, we must have an unwavering trust in God. And to move in that level of trust, we must know God and understand His ways; and to be able to understand the ways of God, we have to hear from Him— *"For the LORD gives wisdom; from his mouth come knowledge and understanding"* (Proverbs 2:6).

But the question is, *"Whom will he teach knowledge? And whom will he make to understand the message? Those just weaned from milk? Those just drawn from the breasts* (Isaiah 28:9)? No, divine wisdom belongs to those who are mature; those who have such an understanding of the kingdom of God that they are willing to give up everything to possess its righteousness and power.

This is one of the main reasons hearing from God is not cheap. It requires a complete investment of ourselves to want to hear from God. It is a daily exercise of our will to choose to pursue God's most precious inheritance: divine wisdom—the word that proceeds out of His mouth.

In Proverbs 8, the Spirit of Divine wisdom, which is a figure of Christ himself, passionately invites men to desire and pursue him. But just as he is eager to entrust us with his treasures, he requires us to be equally passionate to desire what he is offering us:

> I love those who love me, and those who *seek me diligently* will find me (v.17).

> Blessed is the man who listens to me, *watching daily* at my gates, waiting at the posts of my doors (v.34).

From the above Scriptures and several others we have already reviewed, we conclude that spiritual violence is what one does to oneself (the losing of one's life) to possess the life of God. In this sense, violence is positive and indicates the passion involved in giving of oneself to pursue God's will.

Violence in the world, on the other hand, is a perversion by Satan of what God intended for man. In the world, violence is passion directed at robbing other people of their lives to benefit the perpetrator.

Spiritual Violence in Illustration

Chapter 28 of the Book of Job shows us God's requirement for us to access divine wisdom. In my opinion, this chapter illustrates the concept of spiritual violence more vividly than any other Scripture of the bible. It describes the lengths and depths men will go to, and the risks they will take to discover precious metals embedded in the far recesses of the earth. The question then becomes, how far will men go to get divine wisdom from God, which is far more precious than anything man can imagine?

Let us look at Job 28 in its entirety—this is the illustration of spiritual violence:

> People know how to mine silver and refine gold. They know how to dig iron from the earth and smelt copper from stone. They know how to put light into darkness and explore the farthest, darkest regions of

the earth as they search for ore. They sink a mine shaft into the earth far from where anyone lives. They descend on ropes, swinging back and forth. Bread comes from the earth, but below the surface the earth is melted as by fire.

People know how to find sapphires and gold dust—treasures that no bird of prey can see, no falcon's eye observe—for they are deep within the mines. No wild animal has ever walked upon those treasures; no lion has set his paw there. People know how to tear apart flinty rocks and overturn the roots of mountains. They cut tunnels in the rocks and uncover precious stones. They dam up the trickling streams and bring to light the hidden treasures.

But do people know where to find wisdom? Where can they find understanding? No one knows where to find it, for it is not found among the living. 'It is not here,' says the ocean. 'Nor is it here,' says the sea.

It cannot be bought for gold or silver. Its value is greater than all the gold of Ophir, greater than precious onyx stone or sapphires. Wisdom is far more valuable than gold and crystal. It cannot be purchased with jewels mounted in fine gold. Coral and valuable rock crystal are worthless in trying to get it. The price of wisdom is far above pearls. Topaz from Ethiopia cannot be exchanged for it. Its value is greater than the purest gold.

But do people know where to find wisdom? Where can they find understanding? For it is hidden from the eyes of all humanity. Even the sharp-eyed birds in the sky cannot discover it. But Destruction and Death say, 'We have heard a rumor of where wisdom can be found.'

God surely knows where it can be found, for he looks throughout the whole earth, under all the Heavens. He made the winds blow and determined how much rain should fall. He made the laws of the rain and prepared a path for the lightning. Then, when he had done all this, he saw wisdom and measured it. He established it and examined it thoroughly. And this is what he says to all humanity: 'the fear of the LORD is true wisdom; to forsake evil is real understanding.'" (NLT)

The above passage is remarkable in what it implies regarding the discussion in this book so far. This is why we reproduce the entire chapter here. Besides illustrating what it would take to discover divine wisdom, it also raises several rhetorical questions. But, in the end, it only shows the reader the way to the answers, not the answers themselves.

To fully comprehend why God requires self-sacrifice to appropriate divine wisdom, and to understand why Job 28 is so relevant to what we have been saying so far, we need to establish that the wisdom and understanding that is talked about in the passage is the same as the word of God, which we characterize as divine wisdom.

Understanding Divine Wisdom

We learned in previous chapters that the word of God is the essence of God Himself. Now we go further to say that the essence of the word of God is wisdom, understanding and knowledge. In other words, when the word of God comes to us, it is wisdom, understanding and knowledge that come to us. All three constitute divine wisdom. They are not different concepts, but rather differing degrees of divine wisdom. They are so closely related that it is virtually impossible to define any one of them without talking about the others. With that constraint in mind, let us attempt to separate them for the purpose of understanding divine wisdom.

Wisdom in its purest sense talks about the *approach* we have about anything in life. It is about the *skill* we use to navigate life. The Hebrew word translated *wisdom* in Job 28 is *chokmah*, which means skillful or wit. It is derived from the root word *chakam*, which also means to be wise in mind, word or act. So to have wisdom is to have the skill to speak or act appropriately as the occasion of life demands.

Hence, people that have wisdom are able to assess a situation accurately, and tailor their words or action to obtain the best results. It does not mean that wise people know how their words or actions will achieve the result they are seeking. Neither do they know with certainty if their decision will achieve the results intended. They simply have the skill to act appropriately in the particular situation. In modern vernacular, such people have *good sense*.

Understanding is insight gained as a result of thoughtful analysis. The Hebrew word used in Job 28 is *biynah,* which means, *meaning*. It comes from a root, *biyn,* which also means, *to separate mentally, to distinguish*. 'Understanding' is a step removed from the *wisdom* we defined above. It is *wisdom* with a depth to it. To have understanding of a matter is not only to have the skill to speak or to act appropriately in the matter, but to also know why our words or actions will achieve the results intended. If we know why, we also have more confidence to implement our decision.

Proverbs 24:3 shows that understanding builds on wisdom and is deeper. *"Through wisdom a house is built, and by understanding it is established"*.

Wisdom always precedes understanding, because it is the foundation upon which understanding is built. Therefore, Proverbs 4:7 says: *"Wisdom is the principal thing; therefore get wisdom. And in all your getting, get understanding."* The word *principal* in Proverb 4:7 means *first* or *foremost*. Thus, it is possible, although rare, to have wisdom and still lack understanding. But it is impossible to have understanding without wisdom, because, as Proverbs 24:3 implied, you cannot establish what you have not first built.

Another thing to note is that whereas wisdom can come to us intuitively, understanding requires self-investment. This notion is implied in Proverbs 3:13: "Happy is the man who *finds* wisdom, and the man who **gains** understanding. *Finding* can be instantaneous, but *gaining* results from a process over time. Hence, Proverbs 4:1 says, *"Give attention to know understanding"*.

For this reason, understanding is received mostly through meditation. Meditation is a mental activity where we turn over repeatedly the word we receive from God to gain more insight. So what we hear from God is *wisdom,* but the insight we gain from meditating on the word we heard is *understanding.*

Knowledge is the highest level of divine wisdom; thus, it is on a higher plane than understanding. *Knowledge* is an awareness that one acquires as a result of an intimate experience or divine revelation. It is wisdom and understanding rolled into one, and then more. Therefore to have *knowledge* is to have wisdom and understanding at the same time. The word *knowledge,* as described here, is derived from the Hebrew word *yada,* which translates into, among other things, *ascertain by seeing.*

Several other Hebrew and Greek words also translate into *knowledge,* but what we are describing here is the knowledge of the things of God. The corresponding Greek word in the New Testament is *epignosis,* which means to have *full* discernment. *Epignosis* is derived from *epiginosko,* which also means *to become fully acquainted with.*

Therefore *knowledge* is intelligence derived from a personal relationship. It is exactly as the Hebrew and Greek definitions imply: you *know* because you have seen it or have become acquainted with it before. Knowledge beautifies the house that *wisdom* built and *understanding* established in Proverbs 24:3-4:

> Through wisdom a house is built, and by under-standing it is established; by **knowledge** the rooms are filled with all precious and pleasant riches.

Notice that *knowledge* completes the house that wisdom started.

The Greek word *ginosko* properly carries the meaning implied in the phrase, *knowledge of God. Ginosko* means *to know absolutely* or *to be sure.* For us to *ginosko,* God has to impart understanding to us at a deeper level, either through revelation, or through experience.

So the understanding that enables us to know the things of God is not defined by the typical Greek usages, which are all at a comparatively shallower level of natural intelligence. To fully understand the things of God, we need *dianoia,* which translates *deep thought. Dianoia is a* compound word from *'dia'* (channel) and *'nous'* (intellect or mind—divine or human). This *deep thought* has to be at the spirit level, because, according to 1 Corinthians 2:5, the natural man cannot receive spiritual things.

Therefore, when Paul was praying for the Ephesians Church to receive knowledge of their spiritual inheritance in God, the Greek word for *understanding* he uses is *dianoia* not just *nous* or *biynah*:

> ...That the God of our Lord Jesus Christ, the Father of Gory, may give to you the spirit of wisdom and revelation in the knowledge of Him, the eyes of your *understanding* being enlightened; that you may *know* what is the hope of His calling what are the riches of the glory of His inheritance in the saints and what is the exceeding greatness of His power toward us who believe, according to the working of His mighty power (Ephesians 1:17).

Paul's desire in the above Scripture is that God would illuminate that faculty in the believers which was the channel for receiving divine intelligence. This implies that, there is a channel within the spirit of man for receiving divine intelligence, and that God, at His discretion, can sensitize this channel by flooding it with light to enable it to receive revelation.

This revelation imparts to man the knowledge of God's will, and activates man's faith to take action for God. This notion affirms our earlier statement that we cannot hear from God unless He opens our ears to hear.

To summarize, *knowledge* is *understanding* that goes beyond a mere mental process. A person who *knows* has both wisdom and understanding at the same time. Although man generally *knows* through experience, he can also *know* by revelation from God. I believe God imparts *knowledge* to us by both means, because they are both profitable for different purposes.

Knowledge that comes only by revelation can puff up a person— *"Knowledge puffs up, but love edifies"* (I Corinthians 8:1). However, *knowledge* that is the result of experience is more likely to humble the person exercised by it. In the book of Job, God's own testimony to Satan was that Job was perfect, and there was no one in the earth like him (see Job 1:8). Yet God imparted knowledge to him not by revelation alone but by experience also.

God's True Riches: Wisdom, Understanding and Knowledge

This brings us back to Job 28. We learned in that passage that wisdom is far more precious than anything man strives for in this world. But only God knows where to find wisdom.

The rhetorical question becomes, if men will risk their lives for something that is so insignificant compared to wisdom, what will men give to obtain the priceless wisdom of God. To get to this wisdom of God will demand probing depths quite unfamiliar to man because, as Job 28 said about divine wisdom, *"No one knows where to find it, for it is not found among the living."*

An interesting thought in that passage is: *"But do people know where to find wisdom? Where can they find understanding? For it is hidden from the eyes of all humanity."* Why are wisdom, understanding and, by implication, knowledge of God hidden from all humanity? Because, they are the true riches in God's universe! And far beyond that, they are the means by which God has ordained for us to partake of His divine nature (2 Peter 1:2-4).

By wisdom, understanding and knowledge of God, believers can do awesome things in the world. Therefore, God has made it impossible for any person to obtain divine wisdom without first having an intimate covenant relationship with Him.

According to Job 28, divine wisdom is hidden from the eyes of all humanity, and that only God knows where to find it. The reason God is the only one who knows where to find divine wisdom is because He Himself is the source of it: *"For the Lord gives wisdom; from His mouth come knowledge and understanding"* (Proverbs 2:6).

This is why the starting point to obtaining divine wisdom and knowledge is the *fear* of God: *"The fear of the Lord is the beginning of wisdom"* (Psalm 111:10, Proverbs 9:10). And also, *"The fear of the Lord is the beginning of knowledge..."* (Proverbs 1:7)

'The fear of the Lord' is a spiritual concept that describes an attitude of great reverence a person adopts towards God, such that the person is totally disposed to obeying whatever God's says to do. It is the attitude the Bible describes of those *"who tremble at His word"* (Isaiah 66:5).

God created the earth using divine wisdom, and He is willing to share His wisdom with those who fear Him. Listen to Proverbs 3:19 and 20: *"The Lord by wisdom founded the earth; by understanding He established the Heavens; by His knowledge the depths were broken up, and clouds drop down the dew."* Now compare that Scripture with Psalm 33:6: *"By the word of the Lord the Heavens were made, and all the host of them by the breath of His mouth."*

Notice that the *wisdom, understanding* and the *knowledge* that God used to *found the earth* and *establish the Heavens* as revealed in Proverbs 3:19 are equated to the *word* of the Lord that made the Heavens in Psalm 33:6. Therefore the word that proceeds out of the mouth of God is also, at the same time, wisdom, understanding and knowledge.

Consequently, because man can accomplish incredible things with God's word, God releases His word to only those who are mature, and whom He can trust—those in covenant relationship with Him. God presents Jesus to us as the best example of one who had such a covenant relationship with Him. Therefore, God endowed Jesus with the Spirit without limit according to the Scriptures (John 3:34—NIV).

Isaiah 11:2 foretold what God meant by the *Spirit without limit:*

> The Spirit of the Lord shall rest upon Him, the Spirit
> of *wisdom* and *understanding*, the Spirit of counsel
> and might, the Spirit of *knowledge* and of the fear of
> the Lord.

The above passage implies that divine wisdom will be available to us based on the measure of the Holy Spirit in us. Is not this notion consistent with the fact that it is the Holy Spirit who will lead us into all truth (John 16:13); and that the truth we know will set us free (John 8:32)?

We now understand how *wisdom, understanding* and *knowledge*, together, constitute divine wisdom, which we defined as the word that proceeds out of God's mouth. Therefore, because God gave Jesus the Spirit of wisdom, understanding and knowledge, we can assume that whatever Jesus said came directly from God's mouth. This is Jesus' own testimony in John 14:10 regarding this assumption:

> The words that I speak to you I do not speak on My own authority; but the Father who dwells in Me does the works.

That is why Jesus was able to do all the great things He did. He did not do great things because He was God, but rather because he was endowed with divine wisdom, as the Son of God.

Understanding Releases Faith

We will be remiss if we do not mention that faith is a product of understanding, and *great* faith is a product of knowledge. The centurion in Matthew 8:5 had such an understanding and a personal knowledge of how authority works that he was also able to exhibit great faith that surprised even Jesus.

Similarly, the great faith exhibited by Daniel, Shadrach, Meshach, and Abednego in the Book of Daniel was the result of their intimate knowledge of God. Right from the beginning of the Book of Daniel, the Holy Spirit was deliberate about letting us know the level of devotion and the intimate relationship these young men had with God. Therefore we are not left to wonder how God would accord such special favor upon these men, when we read about their spectacular deliverance from death.

It is evident then that we cannot conjure up faith beyond our current knowledge of God. Besides, as we have already mentioned, faith is not something we produce on our own. Romans 8:17 says faith comes by hearing the word of God. So it is God who imparts faith to us, as we receive His word; and He imparts it by measure (Romans 12:3), based on our understanding.

We said earlier that understanding, unlike wisdom, is more a product of meditation than just common sense. Therefore there is a requirement of personal investment in order to understand. This thought is the essence of Mark 4:23-25, when Jesus said:

Pay close attention to what you hear. The closer you listen, the more understanding you will be given—and you will receive even more. To those who listen to my teaching, more understanding will be given. But for those who are not listening, even what little understanding they have will be taken away from them (NLT).

It is this understanding that is missing in our faith today. Faith does not stand alone! According to 2 Peter 1:5-7, we are to add to our faith other pertinent qualities, one of which is knowledge. We cannot act on the word of God if we do not know how to apply it. Hebrew 4:2 says the word of God did not profit the Israelites in the wilderness because they did not mix it with faith. That means the Israelites had some faith, but they lacked understanding to apply that faith to realize their destiny.

How do we know they had some faith? Because that was all the business in the wilderness about—to build up their faith for the grand entry into the Promised Land. God implied in Deuteronomy 8:3 that He led them through all the hardships they encountered, so they would learn to trust His word. But when the time for them to put that built-up faith to use, they turn back in fear. Therefore the word of God that was supposed to bring them to the Promised Land did not profit them. Their problem was that, up to the walls of Jericho, they still did not know God as their God.

As Jesus instructs in Mark 4:24-25 quoted above, we have to expend effort to understand the word of God in order for us to *profit* from the word. This is in line with God's instruction to Joshua to meditate day and night in God's law in order for him to have good success.

Let us emphasize here that our knowledge of God will remain shallow unless we develop and maintain an intimate fellowship with Him. We learned in Chapter 3 that the word of God is the essence of God Himself. Thus, meditating in the word is part of our fellowship with God. And the more we pursue this fellowship, the more understanding will be given to us. When our understanding increases, our knowledge of God also deepens. This is where great faith begins to take root.

But as Mark 4:25 states, when we ignore God's word, and do not gain understanding by it, we will lose even the little understanding we originally possessed. In fact, God is demonstrating love when He refuses to release His precious and powerful word to people who would ignore or misuse it. He delays until we are matured enough to handle His word, '*not willing that any should perish*' (see 2 Peter 3:9). Why? Because, as the Israelites learned in the wilderness, and as we will show later, it is not a light responsibility to be entrusted with the word of God.

Friendship with God is the Key to Divine Wisdom

Those who fear God and tremble at His word enter into a higher level of relationship with Him. They are no longer only children of God but also His friends. The privileges of being a friend of God are enviable. One such privilege is that God begins to reveal secrets to you.

What secrets? They are the principles of the kingdom of God— the wisdom by which God gets things accomplished and miracles to happen. God will also disclose to His friends what He is about to do before He does it. Hence the friends of God gain insight into the future, as Abraham was privileged to experience. Moreover, God allows His friends to argue their case before Him, and allows them to temper His judgments through intercession on behalf of the guilty.

Jesus revealed the principles of the kingdom of God to His disciples, because He qualified them to be His friends.

> You are My friends if you do whatever I command
> you. No longer do I call you servants, for a servant
> does not know what his master is doing; but I have
> called you friends, for all things that I heard from My
> Father I have made known to you (John 15:13-15).

Notice that the qualification for becoming a friend of God is clearly stated by Jesus in the Scriptures above: *"You are My friends if you do whatever I command you."* This is the same quality shared by those who *fear* God and *those who tremble at His word,* as we noted earlier. Psalm 25:14 leaves no doubt about this: *"Friendship with the LORD is reserved for those who fear him. With them he shares the secrets of his covenant"* (NLT).

The Hebrew word translated *friendship* in the Psalm 25:14 by the New Living Translation Bible is *sod.* This same word is translated *secret* in several other translations. In fact, both translations are trying to communicate the measure of *intimacy* suggested in *sod.* The word describes the intimacy shared between a company of people who are in close deliberation (according to Strong's Hebrew and Greek dictionary.) By implication, Psalm 25 is saying that God reveals the secrets of His covenant to only those who have an intimate relationship with Him. These are the friends of God, and their privileges are enviable. Psalm 25:12-13 perhaps best summarizes the benefits of qualifying as a friend of God:

> Who is the man that fears the Lord? Him shall He teach in the way He chooses. He himself shall dwell in prosperity, and his descendants shall inherit the earth.

So what would we give to become friends of God? What lengths and depths would we go to obtain the true riches of wisdom, understanding and knowledge of God? This quest is not for the passive or the fearful. God demands aggressive faith or spiritual violence— those who are willing to forsake all to pursue Him; those who do not love their life even unto death.

Yes, pursuing God with all our heart will cost us our lives; but that fact should not be an occasion for mourning. What we suffer is a *temporary affliction*; what we gain is *"a far more exceeding eternal weight of glory"* (2 Corinthians 4:17).

Violence in the Spirit: Relentless Pursuit

The Holy Spirit indicates to us throughout the Scriptures that we can apprehend the kingdom of God and its righteousness only if we are passionate or aggressive for the things of God. This is a fundamental concept in the kingdom of God; and there is no way around it. We must know and accept this if we are to possess all of our inheritance in Christ in this life. The passive, the lukewarm and the slothful are abominable to God in this regard, and they shall never posses the kingdom of God.

I wish there was an easier way to put it; but search the Scriptures and know for certain that this is the only way God has ordained for us to access the riches of His kingdom. And in Chapter 10, we will show why this is the case.

The following Scriptures affirm what we are saying here. They also show us how to be aggressive or violent in the spirit.

> My son, if you receive my words, and treasure my commands within you, so that you *incline* your ear to wisdom, and *apply* your heart to understanding; yes, if you *cry* out for discernment, and *lift* up your voice for understanding, if you *seek* her as silver, and *search* for her as for hidden treasures; then you will understand the fear of the Lord, and find the knowledge of God (Proverbs 2:1-5).

> My son, *give* attention to my words; *incline* your ear to my sayings. *Do not let them depart* from your eyes; *keep* them in the midst of your heart; for they are life to those who find them, and health to all their flesh (Proverbs 4:20-22).

> This Book of *the Law shall not depart from your mouth, but you shall meditate in it day and night*, that you may *observe to do according to all that is written in it*. For then you will make your way prosperous, and then you will have good success (Joshua1:8).

> I love those who *love* me and those who *seek* me *diligently* will find me. Riches and honor are with me, enduring riches and righteousness. ...Blessed is the man who *listens* to me *watching daily* at my

gates, *waiting* at the posts of my doors. For whoever finds me finds life, and obtains favor from the Lord" (Proverbs 8:17-18, 34-35).

The above Scriptures preach by themselves. We have to pursue the things of God with a passion that cannot be quenched by adversity or any other excuses. This was the way Jesus took, as Isaiah had prophesied (Isaiah 50:5-9). This was the way his apostles took; and this was the way all the other faithful martyrs of old took. They were all consumed by the zeal for God's kingdom, and would not compromise their stance, no matter the cost to their personal security (see John 2:15-17).

Be Careful How You Hear
The Breadth of Hearing

In view of the foregoing, it is evident that how much of God's word we hear depends on how much of ourselves we are willing to give to pursue Him. The amount of passion we give to our pursuit of God comes under the principle of sowing and reaping. The Bible is plain: the more we sow, the more we reap—the more we give, the more we receive. So it is with giving of ourselves to God. The more we desire God and pursue Him, the closer He makes Himself available to us, and the more we can hear from Him.

That is why Jesus charged us to be careful how we hear: *"Therefore take heed how you hear. For whoever has, to him more will be given; and whoever does not have, even what he seems to have will be taken from him"* (Luke 8:18). In other words, the more diligence we show in gaining understanding of the word of God that comes to us, the greater the understanding God will impart to us.

God charges us with the responsibility of searching out His word to ascertain His will, and to do something about it. And so in Hebrews 11:6, He declares, *"He is a rewarder of those who diligently seek Him."* This requirement of God for us to seek Him in order to advance in His kingdom is based on the Law of Reciprocity, which we examine in greater detail in the next Chapter.

The Depth of Hearing

On the other hand, our maturity level determines the level of revelation God imparts to us when we seek Him. There are secrets to the power of God, but no amount of diligence will qualify us for some of these secrets if our diligence does not produce maturity in us. We have touched on this concept before, and we repeat it here for greater emphasis: We open ourselves to great frustration if we assume that, because we have pursued God with all our heart, He is obligated to give us His all. Yes, ultimately, He will give us all that is due us, and more.

Out of love, however, He will not give everything immediately because, as we learned earlier, a sharp sword in the hands of a child is a grave danger not only to himself but also to others around him. Yet the same sword in the hand of a mature person can do profitable things.

Maturity is mostly achieved by consistently doing what God says to do. In other words, the mature have learned to obey God in all things. They are those who fear the Lord and tremble at His word.

The Christians at Corinth were, perhaps, passionate in the things of God; and they were rewarded with an abundance of spiritual gifts. But the apostle Paul considered them immature, and their carnality affirmed that assessment. We quoted Paul's reproof of the Corinthians in Chapter 8 to highlight the same truth, and we quote it here again for further insight:

> Dear brothers and sisters, when I was with you I couldn't talk to you as I would to mature Christians. I had to talk as though you belonged to this world or as though you were infants in the Christian life. I had to feed you with milk and not with solid food, because you couldn't handle anything stronger. And you still aren't ready, for you are still controlled by your own sinful desires (I Corinthians 3:1-3 - NLT).

Paul could only feed the believers at Corinth with milk — elementary doctrines — because they were not ready for the meat of the word. The elementary doctrines and principles of God will get us only so far in the spirit. How much spiritual authority a believer can access depends on the depth of divine wisdom that believer has.

In our three-dimensional world, enclosed under the sun, nothing is exactly as it seems. And going behind the scenes to discover the truth requires a level of spiritual sensitivity developed only in the matured and the gifted. Let us say this more forcefully: the spirit world operates solely on legalities, so we better have the word of God richly dwelling in us before we start making declarations we do not fully understand. Listen to Hebrews 5:13 and 14:

> For everyone who partakes only of milk is unskilled
> in the word of righteousness, for he is a babe. But
> solid food belongs to those who are of full age, that
> is, those who by reason of use have their senses exer-
> cised to discern both good and evil.

If all the word we are qualified to partake in is milk, the Bible says we are unskilled in the word of righteousness. We should not go about brandishing the sharp double-edged sword—the word of God— because we may hurt others and ourselves.

Note what the Scripture above said: the mature came to *full age* by *reason of use*. That means these mature believers have practiced the word of God to the point they can now recognize, with little effort, what is of God and what is not. Such people cannot easily be deceived by the devil.

The Burden of Hearing the Word of God

Our passion to pursue God's wisdom should not diminish after we have attained our goal. If we obtain the knowledge of God and do not use it for the purpose for which God sent it to us, that knowledge will only puff us up and invite God's chastisement on us.

God entrusts His word of wisdom to us because He is looking for those who will establish it in the earth. God is looking for His will to be done in the earth as it is done in Heaven. He is looking to empower a few who will forsake their own ambitions to fulfill His desire in the earth. He wants to show Himself strong on behalf of those whose hearts are towards Him.

And as we have seen already, once the word comes out of God's mouth, it cannot return void of its purpose. Either God gets His purpose done through us or over on top of us; but He will get His purpose accomplished one way or the other.

Therefore the person who hears the word of God carries a great responsibility as well as a great authority to fulfill that responsibility. God's word is so precious in His sight that He will not allow anyone to trifle with it. When God reveals truth to us, He also holds us accountable for that truth; and the believer who trifles with the word of God also suffers a great deal in life.

This was why the Israelites suffered so much in their journey through the wilderness. After they promised God they would listen to whatever He commanded them through Moses, they turned around and murmured, argued, and disobeyed God all the way. And none of those who did so made it to the Promised Land. So again, He warns us in Hebrews 3:15 and 4:7: *"Today, if you will hear His voice, do not harden your hearts as in the rebellion."*

Isaiah 50 describes prophetically the passion of the Messiah to carry out God's will once He came to know it:

> The Sovereign LORD has spoken to me, and I have listened. I do not rebel or turn away. I give my back to those who beat me and my cheeks to those who pull out my beard. I do not hide from shame, for they mock me and spit in my face. Because the Sovereign LORD helps me, I will not be dismayed. Therefore, I have set my face like a stone, determined to do his will. And I know that I will triumph. He who gives me justice is near. Who will dare to oppose me now? Where are my enemies? Let them appear! See, the Sovereign LORD is on my side! Who will declare me guilty? All my enemies will be destroyed like old clothes that have been eaten by moths (Isaiah 50:5-9 - NLT)!

This Scripture is prescriptive in what stance we ought to take when the word of God comes to us. Notice the determination of the

Messiah in the face of adversity and opposition from His enemies. He will not back down at any price. In fact, He dares His enemies to bring it on, being fully assured that God will deliver Him.

Isaiah 50:5-9 also implies that when we are entrusted with the word of God, we will face persecution from the enemy. Many who are unprepared for this type of trial are likened by Jesus in Mark 4:16-17 as:

> These likewise are the ones sown on stony ground who, when they hear the word, immediately receive it with gladness; and they have no root in themselves, and so endure only for a time. Afterward, when *tribulation or persecution* arises *for the word's sake*, immediately they stumble.

Satan's Great Fear

Note that, in Mark 4:17 shown above, tribulation comes as a result of hearing the word of God. But someone may wonder why does Satan stir up trouble for those who receive the word of God? The obvious answer is that Satan does not want them to succeed. However, he also has a more sinister motive.

Acts 3:21 speaks of Christ remaining in Heaven until *"the times of restoration of all things, which God has spoken by the mouth of all His holy prophets since the world began."* The enemy knows that every purpose of God that gets accomplished in the earth brings him closer to the day of his eternal punishment. That is why he will do everything to make us back down or compromise the word of God.

May I also suggest that God will allow the enemy to buffet us if we ignore or procrastinate on His word to us, perhaps, for the same reason Satan fears? God used persecution to scatter the early believers in the book of Acts, because they procrastinated in carrying out Jesus' command to preach the gospel beyond Jerusalem.

I do not believe the devil can do anything to a child of God without God's purpose in it. If the devil could have his way, none of God's children would be alive today.

The story of the prophet Jonah is a classic example of God using tribulations to make us willing to obey His word. What about the freedom of self-determination God gave man? Are we not at liberty to choose to do or not to do God's will? Yes, but that was in regard to salvation. Once we choose God's offer of salvation in Christ, we become a citizens of God's kingdom. And in a kingdom, all citizens are subject to the word of the king.

Besides, we voluntarily relinquish our privilege of freedom when we pursue God with all our heart in order to gain His true riches. We promise through our passionate pursuit that we would become responsible stewards of God's word. This is what Jesus implied in His statement: *"If anyone desires to come after Me, let him deny himself, and take up his cross daily, and follow me"* (Luke 9:23).

"If anyone desires" speaks to our liberty to choose. Notice God is not making anyone do anything. We choose to submit our freedom under God's will in following the Lord.

This makes logical sense. No employer would hire a person who does not share the vision of that employer. We certainly cannot serve two masters, and be faithful to both of them at the same time—we cannot serve God and ourselves at the same time.

So God says, if you want to be in His kingdom, the position of king is already taken. There is only one head from whom all visions flow, and to whom everyone in the kingdom is accountable. And to demonstrate that such an arrangement is actually for the benefit of the citizens of His kingdom, God has promised abundant rewards to all those who give of themselves freely.

Having clarified that, we must also remind ourselves that God owns everything He created, including mankind—both believers and unbelievers. This was the point in Paul's argument in Romans 9:14-18:

What shall we say then? Is there unrighteousness with God? Certainly not! For He says to Moses, 'I will have mercy on whomever I will have mercy, and I will have compassion on whomever I will have compassion.' So then it is not of him who wills, nor of him who runs, but of God who shows mercy. For the Scripture says to the Pharaoh, 'For this very purpose I have raised you up, that I may show My power in you, and that My name may be declared in all the earth.' Therefore He has mercy on whom He wills, and whom He wills He hardens.

The implication in the above Scripture is that God can do anything with anyone whenever He chooses. Even Satan is God's devil! Even so, God allows us the privilege to choose to do His will. However, just as Adam was given a choice and a consequence for that choice, so the consequences of our choices are clearly spelled out by Jesus in Luke 9:24: *"For whoever desires to save his life will lose it, but whoever loses his life for My sake will save it."*

What God is saying in all these Scriptures is that man has a choice to control his own destiny; but there is only one good choice, and that is His appointed destiny. This is God's message to man throughout history. Adam was presented with all the trees in the Garden of Eden but was warned that not all the trees are beneficial to him. Israel was presented with life and death, but admonished to choose life. Today, God continues to warn us: *"...if you hear His word, do not harden your heart"*(Hebrews 4:7).

The Rewards of Obedience

The foregoing section may seem to have ended on a heavy note. This can discourage some people who may feel inadequate to pay so great a price to pursue the kingdom of God. But feeling insufficient to carry the responsibility of God's word does not necessarily indicate a believer is weak or immature. Many great people in the Bible initially felt that way when God called them to carry His purpose. In fact, if the calling of God does not overwhelm us, we may fall into the temptation of carrying it with our own strength. That is why the weight seems so heavy when we think about carrying God's burden.

Nevertheless Christ says His yoke is easy, and His burden is light. So He encourages us to choose His yoke rather than the yoke of this world, which is deceptively easy, but in the end, burns right through your soul.

Paul carried one of the greatest responsibilities for God, faced some of the toughest tribulations, and yet was able to say his afflictions were light and momentarily (2 Corinthians 4:17). His secret was his complete dependence on God to carry that burden. Otherwise, Paul could not have survived his journey in God.

But beyond God helping us to carry His yoke, He has great rewards for those who trust Him enough to accept and fulfill His calling. We can fill the rest of this book with the array of promises God has made to all His faithful servants, but Jesus summarized them all in the following verse:

> And everyone who has left houses or brothers or sisters or father or mother or wife or children or lands, for My name's sake, shall receive a hundred-fold, and inherit eternal life." (Matthew 19:29)

Here also is Paul's exposition on the subject of reward:

> "Our present troubles are quite small and won't last very long. Yet they produce for us an immeasurably great glory that will last forever! So we don't look at the troubles we can see right now; rather, we look forward to what we have not yet seen. For the troubles we see will soon be over, but the joys to come will last forever (2 Corinthians 4:17, 18 - NLT).

And 2 Corinthians 2:9 neatly binds them all together:

> No eye has seen, no ear has heard, and no mind has imagined what God has prepared for those who love him (NLT).

God wants to demonstrate His glory to the world through us, and He is paying handsomely for those who will heed His call. God could do it all by Himself, if He so chooses; but out of His infinite love, He has decided to include man to share in both the price and the prize.

If we focus only on the price we miss the better part. The Bible says Jesus endured the cross because He set His eyes on *the joy that was set before Him* (Hebrews 12:2). So let us also keep our focus on the incredible prize, and all the afflictions we have to endure will seem light and momentary, as the apostle Paul also came to realize.

When we are born again, we gain legal access into the New Covenant of God that was put into effect through the blood of Jesus. As we learned earlier, our inheritance under this New Covenant is that God becomes our God, and we become God's people. Possessing God as our God is an enormous wealth, as we have discovered throughout this book.

Nevertheless, we do not automatically receive the benefits of the kingdom of God merely because we are God's people. The afflictions, the persecutions and the pressures we endure to possess the kingdom of God become the sacrifice by which we enter into the greater privileges of the covenant of God (see Psalm 50:5 and Acts 14:22).

The highest privilege awaiting those who trust and diligently seek after God is *friendship* with Him. We briefly talked about this privilege, when we discussed the passion required to access the things of God. Abraham had a taste of this prize when God told him in Genesis 15:1, *"I am your exceedingly great reward."* In that reward is everything our minds cannot fathom: God as our friend, partner, confidant, defense and provider.

Friendship with God is a walk and an intimacy with the abiding presence of the Lord. The benefits are indescribable: *"In Your presence is fullness of joy; at Your right hand are pleasures forever more"* (Psalm 16:11). Moses understood the blessing of the presence of God so much that he asked God to abort the journey to the Promised Land, when God threatened He would no longer go with them. But because he was a friend of God, God had to oblige him, and withdraw His threat.

Also, the friends of God become privy to advance notice of what God is about to do in the earth. Psalm 25:14 says, *"The secret of the Lord is with them that fear Him..."* This is why God could not keep His plan to destroy Sodom and Gomorrah from Abraham, who God describes as His friend (Genesis 18:17). We saw in the example of Moses given above, the friends of God are also privileged to influence the mind of God through intercession—What a great honor for those who are able to attain unto this privilege!

183

CHAPTER 10

THE LAW OF RECIPROCITY

Do not be deceived, God is not mocked; for whatever a man sows, that he will also reap. For he who sows to his flesh will of the flesh reap corruption, but he who sows to the Spirit will of the Spirit reap everlasting life. And let us not grow weary while doing good, for in due season we shall reap if we do not lose heart (Galatians 6:7-9).

We have so far demonstrated that, in order for God to entrust His precious word—divine wisdom—to us, we must choose to pursue Him with all our heart. And setting ourselves to seek the face of God daily is our demonstration of this diligent pursuit. Thus, everything we have said in this book speaks to one conclusion: we must *seek* God to know and to establish his will in the earth.

But one may wonder, why does God require us to seek Him first for Him to show us His will? Why does He sometimes appear to hide from us, when He could be available to us any moment He chooses? The answer is in understanding the phenomenon we aptly call, the *Law of Reciprocity*—a fundamental law in the kingdom of God that regulates virtually every activity in the universe. In fact, it is this law that gives meaning to why God gave man the great privilege of self-determination.

Seeking God is probably the most often repeated commandment of God in the Bible. The failure of God's people to seek Him is also the number one lamentation of God. But the puzzling question remains, why does an all-sufficient God desire for man to seek Him? By all accounts in the Book of Revelation, God is never lonely, being surrounded by all the angels and elders that worship Him day and night without ceasing. That makes it even more perplexing why God would even seek man's worship. God can have anything He wants just by speaking it into being. So it is obvious there must be a spiritual logic for God to require man to seek Him. That logic is in the law of reciprocity, which we will describe shortly.

We have already seen that, generally, God does not speak to people indiscriminately. We learned this was because of the potency of God's word and the responsibility and faithfulness required to be a steward of His precious word. We also learned that because man must exercise his freedom of choice in order to achieve dominion in the earth, nothing in the kingdom of God is automatic to man.

Man must exercise his will to choose God's will. Man must first acknowledge that he has freedom to choose, and demonstrate that he voluntarily submits to the will of God in love. Therefore the act of seeking God represents our willingness to submit our freedom to choose God's way instead of pursuing our own way. It is our expression of faith in God's authority and wisdom in the governance of the universe.

I believe this concept bears repeating: Because man was created to be like God, man is sovereign over his own destiny, and God will never violate that sovereignty for all eternity. God can make us *willing* to obey Him (see Ephesians 2:13) by using all kinds of motivations. This He does in all His children out of love, because He knows that His way is the only way to the abundant life that He so yearns for His children to enjoy.

And depending on the significance of the purpose at stake, the motivation He uses to get us to choose His way can be equally significant. Great examples of God's heavy hand prodding us to choose His way can be found in the stories of the prophet Jonah and the conversion of the apostle Paul.

However, it is crucial to understand that God is not asking man to *surrender* his freedom in choosing His will. God gave man sovereignty (which equates to man's legitimate exercise of his will for his own end) for a reason, and the notion of *surrendering* one's will to God is very unfortunate. Yes, it sounds very spiritual, but it is not scriptural. Yes, we have hymns urging us to *'surrender all'* to Jesus, but it still contradicts God's will for us. What God teaches is *submission* to His will, and that is completely different from *surrendering* our will.

The concept of *surrender* implies we are no longer in charge of our will and that, somehow, we now become like puppets in the hands of God, where He pulls the strings and we act accordingly. NO! By submitting to God, we are *choosing* to align our will with His will. We point our will in the same direction as God's will; ultimately, His will becomes our will. There is no surrender here. When all is said and done, we still have full control of our will; only its nature or inclination has changed.

The concept of surrender is appropriate only in a circumstance where one is forced to give up resistance because of imminent defeat. But God is not at war with us seeking our defeat and surrender. In fact, nowhere in the Bible is the word *surrender* used to describe God's relationship with man. Interestingly, the Bible documents that, whenever God's people failed to *submit* to Him, they ended up *surrendering* to their enemies.

The reason this distinction is so important and worth this digression is that many of God's people have misunderstood God's purpose in submission, and have surrendered their will to become totally powerless in the kingdom of God. Such people live a life of passivity, and are always waiting for God to do something for them, because now, they reason, they no longer own their will.

No, God will never take over man's will. That is what demons try to do to ignorant people. That is what witchcraft is all about. We may, perhaps, make a dubious exception in our disagreement over the usage of *'surrender'* only at the point of salvation, when a sinner could be said to have surrendered to the love of God. But after we are born again, God works *through* us and not *in place of* us! Remember His proclamation regarding Adam and Eve: *"Let them* *have dominion"* (Genesis 1:26). It is man's responsibility to exercise dominion in the earth.

Therefore, when we *seek* God, we are demonstrating our willingness to submit to His will. And when we do, God responds by working with us and through us to accomplish His will in the earth. Then, He is also able to reward us accordingly as He promised. This is the reason we have to acknowledge God in all our ways for Him to be involved in our decisions.

The Workings of the Law of Reciprocity

It is the dynamics of action and a reciprocate response between God and His creation that sets in motion the *Law of Reciprocity*. This law is the energy that drives every activity in the kingdom of God. Therefore the Law of Reciprocity reverberates in everything in the universe.

It is the law of cause and effect. Every cause produces an effect; every action generates a reaction. This is also the law that underlies the seed-harvest principle, as Paul enunciated so eloquently in Galatians 6:7-9, quoted at the beginning of this chapter. It is a fundamental law that governs everything, good or bad; and we shall do well to understand and harness its possibilities to establish God's kingdom in the earth.

The bible is filled with the essence of the law of reciprocity and we quote a few here:

> To the faithful you show yourself faithful; to those with integrity you show integrity. To the pure you show yourself pure, but to the wicked you show yourself hostile (Psalm 18:25-26—NLT).

> Draw near to God and He will draw near to you (James 4:8).

> Do good, O Lord, to those who are good, and to those who are upright in their hearts (Psalm 125:4).

The Lord is near to all who call upon Him, to all who call upon Him in truth. He will fulfill the desire of those who fear Him; He also will hear their cry and save them. The Lord preserves all who love Him... (Psalm 145:18-20).

As he loved cursing, so let it come to him; as he did not delight in blessing, so let it be far from him (Psalm 109:17).

As for such as turn aside to their crooked ways, the Lord shall lead them away with the workers of iniquity (Psalm 125:5).

...Because you have rejected knowledge, I also will reject you from being priest for Me; Because you have forgotten the law of your God, I also will forget your children (Hosea 4:6).

Since they refused to listen when I called to them, I would not listen when they called to me, says the LORD Almighty (Zechariah 7:13—NLT).

They have roused my jealousy by worshiping non-gods; they have provoked my fury with useless idols. Now I will rouse their jealousy by blessing other nations; I will provoke their fury by blessing the foolish Gentiles (Deuteronomy 32:21—NLT)

If you give, you will receive... Whatever measure you use in giving—large or small—it will be used to measure what is given back to you (Luke 6:38—NLT).

But this I say: He who sows sparingly will also reap sparingly, and he who sows bountifully will also reap bountifully (2Corinthians 9:6).

Virtually all the beatitudes taught by Jesus in Matthew 5 demonstrated the Law of Reciprocity:

> Blessed are the meek, for they shall inherit the earth. Blessed are those who hunger and thirst for righteousness, for they shall be filled. Blessed are the merciful, for they shall obtain mercy. Blessed are the pure in heart, for they shall see God. Blessed are the peacemakers, for they shall be called sons of God. Blessed are those who are persecuted for righteousness' sake, for theirs is the kingdom of Heaven (vs. 5-10)

We repeat: all activities in the universe are governed by the law of reciprocity. God reaffirmed this principle after the flood in Noah's day saying:

> While the earth remains seedtime and harvest... will never cease." (Genesis 8:22.)

The Four Attributes of the Law of Reciprocity

Four things can be gleaned from Genesis 8:22 above and Galatians 6:7-9 we quoted at the beginning of this chapter. First, the phrase, *"While the earth remains"* in Genesis 8:22, tells us that the law governing seedtime and harvest is a permanent law. Because, according to Psalm 78:69, God has established the earth to last forever. Therefore, the law of reciprocity, reflected in the principle of sowing and reaping, is established in the earth forever.

Consequently, all dealings of God with man in the earth are influenced by this seed-harvest principle. (The earth being established to last forever and the world coming to an end, as the Scriptures reveal, are two different concepts, the discussion of which is beyond the scope of this book.)

Whatever God says or releases to man, God requires a response from man; whatever response man gives God, God reciprocates in kind. These reciprocal exchanges between man and God are leading to something wonderful in the plan of God: that the earth will ultimately mirror Heaven. And this is exactly what Jesus taught us to pray for every day: *"Your will be done on earth as it is in Heaven"* (Matthew 6:10).

Galatians 6:8-9 covers the remaining three attributes of the Law of Reciprocity. The second attribute to note is that the law works both in the natural and in the spirit, hence, *"... he who sows to his flesh... but he who sows to the Spirit..."*

It would be superfluous to attempt to describe how man's actions on planet earth have resulted in the conundrums he finds himself today. The evidence of the Law of Reciprocity is obvious for all to see in the corruption and the blessing that surround us daily in the earth. And of course, every Christian must know by now how our actions produce spiritual consequences in our lives.

Thirdly, the law works both for good and for evil: *"...will reap corruption... will reap everlasting life."* The evidence of corruption and blessing suggested in the second attribute we discussed above also illustrates the negative and positive connotations of the Law of Reciprocity.

And lastly, there is a *due season* for each harvest, consequence or reaction to manifest: *"...for in due season we shall reap..."* Some consequences are experienced immediately; others take time to manifest, while the consequences of some more serious sins are reserved for the Day of Judgment, when God will judge every deed of man.

Presently, we do not know all the principles that govern the time span for the consequence of each reciprocate action to manifest. For instance, someone may commit a robbery for the first time and get arrested or killed in the process. Yet other robbers, who have been stealing most of their lifetime, may continue to live a long time on their ill-gotten wealth without any apparent repercussions. Because every thing in the universe is subject to the word of God, we can speculate that there are other laws that regulate these consequences.

We may infer a fifth attribute implicit in Galatians 6:7-8 and Genesis 8:22 regarding the seed-harvest principle. This attribute is also explicitly taught and demonstrated throughout the Scriptures. It is the concept of bountiful return on the seed. In other words, every seed sown returns in multiplied form, as a harvest—that is, the harvest is always greater than the seed!

You've Got To Hear From God And It's Not Cheap

This potential in a seed to yield a bountiful harvest, we will show, reflects God's loving nature, and His passion to bless man. And as we have already shown through Genesis 5:29, all of God commands to us are aimed at giving us this bountiful return, when we obey God.

God as the First Cause in the Law of Reciprocity

Here is an important truth relating to the law of reciprocity: God is the only legitimate first cause of all things. In other words, God is the initiator of all the exchanges involved in the law of reciprocity. So when God instructs us to give or sow a seed, it is because He has first given unto us something to give.

To illustrate, it is God who first gives seed to the farmer, and the farmer responds by planting the seed. Then God causes the seed to multiply for a harvest, and the farmer acknowledges God in thanksgiving, to which God responds with more seed, and the cycle continues (See 2 Corinthians 9:10, Isaiah 55:10 and Malachi 3:10).

Also, when God says, "praise or worship me as God", it is because He first elevated us to be gods (Genesis 1:24, Psalm 82:6, John 10:34). When God says, "honor or glorify Me", it is because He first honored us, and crowned us with glory (Psalm 8:5). God is always the Alpha and the Omega; He is also *"the author and finisher of our faith"*, according to Hebrew 12:2. Therefore God cannot bless whatever does not start with Him.

In fact, the Law of Reciprocity generates a negative response in the form of curses and other severe judgments when man assumes the role of the first cause. This is what is described in the Scriptures as: trusting in *"your own understanding"*(Proverb 3:5), taking a *"way that seems right in the eyes of man"* (Proverbs 14:12), and walking in *"the light of your fire"* (Isaiah 50:11).

Thus, when man initiates an action without God's authority, we can expect the law of reciprocity to produce a harvest of curses. This is the basis of the judgment of God. God is love, but He is also a judge; and it is the law of reciprocity that enables Him to exercise both positions at the same time.

Also, as we mentioned briefly earlier, the Law of Reciprocity explains God's passion to command His people to obey His word.

192

Every command or principle we obey allows God to also honor His promise to us. Our failure to obey the word of God also results in the corruption we see around us daily.

Indeed, all of God's commands, statutes, precepts and laws are for the benefit of man. The commands to love, seek, worship and praise God are for the benefit of man and not for God. And they are all leading to one loving expectation of God: that the earth will become as Heaven.

True, God is worthy of all praise, even if there were no benefits to man for praising God. But God does not need our praise and worship to be God. Imagine all the countless number of angels, who obey and worship God without ceasing. Jesus implied in a statement in Luke 19:40 that, even if man would refuse to praise God, the very stones would immediately cry out in praise to Him. Hear this again: God does not *need* man's praise! Rather, man has a need to praise, worship and obey God.

Let me explain further: There are three fundamental principles in the kingdom of God that interact to explain why we need to seek God and obey Him in all things: the law of self-determination, the law of reciprocity and the law of love.

Because man has freedom to choose his own destiny, his dominion in the earth must be exercised through his choices. We have covered this principle of self-determination comprehensively in previous chapters.

The essence of the law of self-determination is that God will only guide us, and react to our choices. Hence, God can only help us if we choose His help. This freedom to choose sets in motion the law of reciprocity, which is exemplified succinctly in James 4:8: *"Draw near to God and He will draw near to you."*

The principle of Love emanates from the fact that God is love. The nature of love is to give of itself. God yearns to share His love with us, but His own law binds His hands. God, as the first cause of all things, will extend His love to man by various actions of blessing. But beyond that, man must choose to respond to God's love in order for God to reciprocate in love again. This means that, if man rejects God's love, God cannot set aside that rejection, and give man the benefit of His love. This constraint is also due to the law of reciprocity.

We have already touched on the above understanding before, but this is one of the fundamental reasons some people will end up in Hell that was not meant for them. God Has provided atonement for all the sins of men; hence, salvation has been earned for all men. And yet, man has to choose God's offer of salvation, else he perishes right before the eyes of God.

The Law of Reciprocity Necessitated the New Covenant

Remember that the ultimate goal of the New Covenant by which we are brought into fellowship with God is that God will be our God, and that we will be His people. But for us to be the people of God, we have to live by the word of God. Therefore, everything God does under the New Covenant is to make us willing to choose to obey His word.

Let us take a fresh look at the essentials of the covenant from Jeremiah 31:33 again:

> This is the covenant I will make with the house of Israel after that time," declares the LORD. I will put my law in their minds and write it on their hearts. I will be their God, and they will be my people...

Then in Ezekiel 36:26-28:

> I will give you a new heart and put a new spirit within you; I will take the heart of stone out of your flesh and give you a heart of flesh. I will put My Spirit within you and cause you to walk in My statutes, and you will keep My judgments and do them. Then you shall dwell in the land that I gave to your fathers; you shall be My people, and I will be your God.

Oh, how I wish God's people would understand His heart for them! God will not violate man's freedom to choose, but His passion for man would not let Him wait for man to choose wrong, whether out of ignorance or stubbornness. Look at Ezekiel 36 above, and see what lengths God is willing to go to make us choose His will. It is as if God is looking for an excuse to shower His love on us. But that is exactly what God is seeking: an opportunity to bless man. And that is the essence of 2 Chronicles 16:9:

> For the eyes of the Lord run to and fro throughout the whole earth, to show Himself strong on behalf of those whose heart is loyal to Him.

Hear this again: God is looking for an opportunity to bless us, but He cannot release His blessing to us, if we do not respond to His love according to His word.

We have looked at Deuteronomy 5:29 more than once before, but listen to it with a fresh insight into the yearnings of God's heart:

> Oh, that they had such a heart in them that they would fear Me and always keep all My commandments, *that it might be well with them and with their children forever* (emphasis added)!

God is not seeking anything for Himself. All that He commands man to do is so that *"it might be well with them and with their children forever!"* Paul was alluding to the same concept, when he wrote in 2 Corinthians 4:15: *"For all things are for your sakes, that grace, having spread through the many, may cause thanksgiving to abound to the glory of God."* Yes, God receives the thanksgiving and the glory for the results, but that is not His primary goal. His prime objective has always been to bless man.

The Psalmist, in Psalm 8:4-5, is overwhelmed by the mere thought of this undeserved favor of God towards man:

> What are mortals that you should think of us, mere humans that you should care for us? For you made us only a little lower than God, and you crowned us with glory and honor – (NLT).

195

What an honor and glory for God to make man a little lower than Himself—above His faithful angels, above all His other excellent creations. Hence, His love for man has always been unconditional. The apostle John could not restrain his gratitude for the same thought, writing in 1 John 3:1, *"Behold what manner of love the Father has bestowed on us, that we should be called children of God!"* All these Scriptures suggest that it is man's choice and ignorance, not God's anger, that put man into trouble, and ultimately into Hell.

Therefore the commandments to worship and praise God, together with all the other spiritual activities we are commanded to obey, are for the benefit of God only insofar as we are blessed through our obedience. As we give of ourselves to God, the Law of Reciprocity dictates that God gives of Himself to us. This, again, is the basic implication of God being our God, and we being His people under the New Covenant.

The Purest Love and the Highest Worship

Here is a secret that should catapult our worship and praise of God to a higher level: The essence of true love is that it gives without expecting benefit for itself. This is the central message of Paul's eloquent exposition of love in 1 Corinthians 13.

Whenever I read that Scripture, I was always perplexed at how much good deeds still did not count as love. The God-kind of love Paul describes in that Scripture is totally selfless.

So when we worship God because we know He is going to bless us for doing so, we violate a principle of love. Love says, "I don't have any selfish motive when I give of myself." The moment the blessing from God becomes the motive for our worship and praise rather than the fact that God, as our creator, savior and our very life, deserves to be praised and worshipped, we reduce our devotion to a manipulative tool to get our desires.

Pure worship should be for the benefit of God as God alone; and when we arrive at this level of worship, the response from God is also abundant and full to overflowing. When the blessing becomes our focus in our worship, we receive just a blessing, and at less than full measure.

196

It seems that God has predicated the entire history of man to bringing man to this level of pure love, which will allow God to reciprocate His full love to man without measure. Or said more accurately, which will allow man to receive the fullness of God's love. God guarantees that He will bring man to this ideal love through the New Covenant, because success of this covenant depends on God alone.

God has first given Himself to man, and by the Law of Reciprocity, He will receive a people who will give Him the opportunity to demonstrate His infinite love towards them. Yes, the length, the breadth and the depth of God's love are beyond measure towards those who reciprocate God's love as promised in 1 Corinthians 2:9:

> Eye has not seen, nor ear heard, nor have entered into the heart of man the things which God has prepared **for those who love Him** (emphasis added).

Therefore, let us follow the counsel of the Psalmist:

> Glory ye in his holy name: let the heart of them rejoice that seek the LORD. Seek the LORD, and his strength: seek his face evermore" (Psalm 105:3, 4).

> The young lions do lack, and suffer hunger: but they that seek the LORD shall not want any good thing" (Psalm 34:10).

When Seeking God is not an Option

We have been able to show that the Law of Reciprocity is the foundational logic for man to seek God. The evidence in the Scriptures is overwhelming that this is the way of the Spirit in all things pertaining to the earth. Hence, seeking God is never an option to a Christian seeking spiritual progress.

But I find it necessary to discuss two special situations where man's need to seek God becomes imperative, and he cannot go any further without resolving that need. The two special circumstances are:

1. Unconfessed or on-going sin.

2. When God earmarks us for spiritual promotion.

Unconfessed Sin

First, sin erects a barrier between us and God as Isaiah 59:1, 2 affirms:

> Behold, the Lord's hand is not shortened, that it cannot save; nor His ear heavy, that it cannot hear. But *your iniquities have separated you from your God*; and *your sins have hidden His face from you*, so that He will not hear.

It is clear then, that sin separates us from God, and hides His face from us. And if we know we have sinned, then here is God's instruction for us to remedy the situation:

> If we confess our sins, He is faithful and just to forgive us our sins and to cleanse us from all unrighteousness (1 John 1:9).

> Seek the Lord while He may be found, call upon Him while He is near. Let the wicked forsake his way and the unrighteous man his thoughts; Let him return to the Lord and He will have mercy on him and to our God, for He will abundantly pardon (Isaiah 55:6-7).

Note that we have to seek the Lord because we are the ones who have departed from His way, and must return to Him. The picture presented in Isaiah 55 quoted above is that, if we continue in our sin, we drift further and further away from God, and finding our way back to Him may not be as easy. That is why we must seek the Lord quickly *"while He is near,"* and *"while He may be found."*

Spiritual Promotion

But other times, God does hide Himself from us on purpose. And when this is the case, it is often His benign way of pushing us to the next level in Him. When God wants to promote us, He can accelerate the promotion by making us ready for that promotion. He causes us to qualify by making us increase our spiritual maturity.

In the case of Job, we know the end results of all the afflictions he went through was that he obtained a higher level of knowledge about God than he had previously. And that higher knowledge, I believe, qualified Job to receive from God two times more than he had lost. In other words, God expanded Job's capacity to receive an expanded blessing by giving Job a deeper knowledge about God. Is this not the same meaning communicated to us in 2 Peter 1:2: that grace and peace are *multiplied* to us through our knowledge of God.

We know Job's afflictions were God's way of getting him to that new level of knowledge about God. But to lead Job to that stage, God had to hide Himself from Job for a season. Job then had to realize the inadequacy of all the previous theologies he had formulated about God. When Job came to the end of all his wits, God came to him with a new revelation about Himself. And here was Job's humble response when he understood the way God had taken him:

> You ask, 'Who is this that questions my wisdom with such ignorance?' It is I. And I was talking about things I did not understand, things far too wonderful for me. "You said, 'Listen and I will speak! I have some questions for you, and you must answer them.' "*I had heard about you before, but now I have seen you with my own eyes*. I take back everything I said… (Job 42:4-5 – NLT).

If God had shown Job this knowledge without letting him first experience the inadequacy of his previous theology about God, Job would simply have added the new revelation to the old theology. And remember what Jesus taught about putting new wine in an old wineskin. In Job's case, confusion of who God really was would have been the result. But the way God took Job produced this result in him: "*I was talking about things I did not understand, things far too wonderful for me … I take back everything I said…*"

The process of God hiding and Job seeking Him produced two effects: First, it allowed Job to realize the inadequacy of his old theology about God; and secondly, it opened him up to new revelation. Job is able to discard his old theology because of the way God took him.

But let us say, we have received forgiveness for all our sins; and let us say, we have obtained a higher level of knowledge of God than we used to have. Would our lack of sin or the attainment of greater knowledge exempt us from seeking God? No, regardless of what level of perfection we attain, our need to seek God daily would never go away. And this, we have already explained, is due to the immutable Law of Reciprocity.

CHAPTER 11

TO OBEY OR NOT TO OBEY

It is perhaps superfluous at this juncture to explain that we can have victory in every circumstance we face. Victory is the only outcome God has ordained for us. And He has removed all excuses from us, because, as His word says, He always causes us to triumph in Christ (2 Corinthians 2:14). Moreover, Jesus' assurance in Mark 11:22-23 does not leave us a single option for failure. He assured us in that Scripture that, if we have faith in God, nothing would be impossible to us.

That leaves only one variable: *us*. We are the only variable that determines the outcomes of God's promises to us. And the only question to be settled in any circumstance we face is whether to snatch victory by faith, or to shrink back in fear and defeat.

If God causes us to triumph always, then it means He holds the secret to the heart of every situation. His word out of His mouth is this secret, and those who have a living relationship with Him know how to access this wealth of wisdom by which everything in creation, including your problem, came to be.

Thus, the pervasive theme running through every chapter of this book has been the understanding that the word of God is the principal thing in the universe; therefore, we must seek God diligently to ensure that we are never without our daily supply of His powerful word.

This knowledge should lead us to an intense and intimate fellowship with God on a daily basis. And if we do this with all of our heart, then God will also respond with all His best—In His presence is fullness of joy; at His right hand are pleasures forevermore.

Our faith alone determines how far we go with God. In fact, it is more likely for you, as the reader, to obtain greater testimonies than I have shared in this book, because you would be starting from a position of more knowledge and understanding.

When I started to walk with God, the only thing I had was a deep hunger to know more about God. Not surprisingly, I made a lot of terrible mistakes, and paid dearly for some of them. God did not shield me from making those mistakes, nor did He save me from all of the consequences of making those mistakes. And this was because He had preordained all of my outcomes to be used for good in His kingdom.

Therefore, if there is any good done through this book, then I thank the Lord for allowing me to learn and grow through my mistakes. I can now say with the Psalmist in Psalm 119:71, *"It is good that I have been afflicted that I might learn to obey all your precepts."*

The word obedience has taken on such a negative connotation that most people resist anything that has an appearance of yielding to another's authority. But like many wonderful things in the world that Satan has corrupted, the requirement for obedience in the kingdom of God is actually the result of God's love.

For instance, parents give their children rules to obey, not because those rules give the parents any sense of pleasure, but because those rules protect the children. Sometimes, a child may wonder why his or her freedom is being curtailed, and may try to avoid the rules. But we, as matured, know that rules do not curtail a child's freedom. In fact, the rules maintain the child's freedom. An unprotected child injured by a dangerous device or activity is now left with one less thing he or she can do because of the injury.

Similarly, man's desire to free his liberty from the laws of God does not result in more freedom but less freedom for him. Just survey your own life over the years, and see how much pain you could have avoided if you had lived only by God's rules. Today, many of us are in various degrees of bondage (less freedom), because we bought into the old lie of Satan that God is trying to deprive us of our freedom by His commandments.

I am concerned that some of us do not seek God's word, because it has become to us a wearisome burden of rules upon rules that have no effect upon our lives. This was the same attitude Israel adopted towards the word of God for which God chastised them. In Isaiah 28:9-10: The people complained:

> "Who is it he is trying to teach"? To whom is he explaining his message? To children weaned from their milk, to those just taken from the breast? For it is: Do and do, do and do, rule on rule, rule on rule, a little here, a little there—(NIV).

So God reciprocated their attitude back to them:

> Very well then, with foreign lips and strange tongues God will speak to this people …So then, the word of the Lord to them will become: Do and do, do and do, rule on rule, rule on rule; a little here, a little there— so that they will go and fall backward, be injured and snared and captured (vs. 11, 13).

Notice that Israel's response to the word of God determined what they received from the word.

In the Scriptures above, Israel saw God's word to them as burdensome and meaningless when, in fact, God's objective was to give them rest by that same word:

> …To whom he said, 'This is the resting place, let the weary rest'; and, 'this is the place of repose'—But they would not listen (v. 12).

Obedience activates the Benefits of the Law of Reciprocity

Due to the attitude of the Israelites, the spiritual Law of Reciprocity ensured that they received out of the word of God exactly what they murmured about. We simply cannot get around the Law of Reciprocity, but we can harness its possibilities for our advantage. How? By trusting and obeying God in everything!

Satan is roaming the earth, roaring like a lion, and seeking whom he may devour (1 Peter 5:8). This adversary has succeeded in creating a system of lies in the world that blinds people from seeing the abundant life God provides in His kingdom. God therefore gives us His laws to protect us from Satan's schemes—just like any good parents would do for their children.

We learned from Isaiah 28:12 above that all the commands of God are intended to bring man to a place of rest from all burdens, and to show man the way to true pleasure and prosperity— just as God intended for Adam and Eve in the beginning. So we have to seek God; we have to hear from God; and we have to choose God's way. Then, by the reciprocating action of God, we shall have the abundant life He promised us—This is the inheritance of every believer.

But as we have seen throughout this book, the disposition to choose God's way is not always easy to cultivate. This is because it requires us to willingly submit our present freedom under God's will in order to obtain the promise of a greater freedom.

This difficulty arises partly because our fallen nature, seeking pleasure for itself, resists any attempt that seems to encroach on its ability to gain pleasure. Therefore, until our minds are renewed to the love of God and to the deception of the enemy, this resistance from our old nature will continue to be a real battle and a stumbling block for us.

Consequently, the Holy Spirit engages us in a life-long process, teaching us the knowledge of God to renew our mind, to manifest God's divine nature in us, and to make our obedience to God our preferred choice in all circumstances. If we submit to His training, then God is able to *legally* reciprocate in an overflowing love towards us, releasing to us His immeasurable riches in Christ.

Since God foreknew us before we showed up in the earth, and all our days were written in His book (Psalm 139:16), it is only wise on our part to seek His face daily to receive wisdom as to how to get to the future He has graciously carved for us. This is what He says to us in Jeremiah 29:11:

> For I know the thoughts that I think toward you, says the Lord, thoughts of peace and not of evil, to give you a future and a hope.

This *future* and *hope* is God's preference for us. But the only way for Him to administer that preference on our behalf is for us to *choose* His preference. Therefore, to obey is the only choice left for us to see His kingdom manifest in our lives and in the world. Or if we so choose, we can disobey, and continue to live in the corruption that surrounds us daily.

I am careful not to commit the mistakes of Job's friends, who sounded like they knew all there was to know about God's ways and dealings with man. I do not for an instant claim that the understanding I bring to the word of God in this book represents the whole counsel of God on any particular subject. But I am confident that it is all in the way of truth. I am trusting that, as you meditate on these truths for yourself, you will be attaining unto higher dimensions of God's infinite wisdom from which some day I in turn hope to benefit. For Ephesians 4:16 says:

> Under his direction, the whole body is fitted together perfectly. **As each part does its own special work, it helps the other parts grow**, so that the whole body is healthy and growing and full of love – NLT (emphasis added).

The Dawning of the Era of the Knowledge of God

Today, we are all standing on the shoulders of greater men who lived in lesser times—those who labored faithfully to lay for us a solid foundation upon which we receive further insight into the wisdom of Christ and of His kingdom. Consequently, we are destined to receive more knowledge of God during our age than has been possible in any past age. The reason for this increasing knowledge in our time is, simply, because God has ordained it to be so. For Habakkuk 2:14 predicts:

> The earth will be filled with the knowledge of the glory of the Lord, as the waters cover the sea.

What is important then is for us to recognize our responsibilities during these times of *knowledge*, and to follow the example of the sons of Issachar in their time. The Bible says they had understanding of the times, to know what Israel ought to do (1 Chronicles 12:32).

We are living in an era variously called the Last Days, the Eleventh Hour, or the End Times. Although many of us are aware of this prophetic era, only a few care enough to find out what the will of God is during this time in history. It appears the enemy has succeeded in entangling many of us in enough personal battles until all we can see is our own predicaments, and how to be free from the daily pressures of life.

But from God's perspective, we are the ornaments He is using to decorate the house that wisdom built, and understanding established in Proverbs 24:3. We are God's master showpiece—the final grand act of the drama of human history. And He is counting on us to reciprocate this undeserved gesture of love by fully cooperating with His Holy Spirit. That is why He asks us to present our bodies as living sacrifices to Him, so that He would find no areas of resistance in us.

The entire creation of God is also waiting for us (see Romans 8:18); all the angel are watching and wondering what the grand plan of God for man is (see 1 Peter 1:12); and the giants of faith mentioned in Hebrews 11 are eagerly awaiting the time they will finally be perfected, as God has decreed that they would not be made perfect without us (Hebrew 11:39).

God wants to exhibit to all His creation, including the principalities and powers of darkness, His manifold wisdom, His unsurpassed glory and power and His unfathomable love. And God wants to achieve the maximum effect of this exhibition by using, arguably, the least qualified of people living in the best and the worst times of history. This is an awesome responsibility for us, and pursuing to know God, and to understand His will is the key to completely discharge this responsibility.

See The Bigger Picture

Therefore, the broader goal of this book is not about pursuing God merely to obtain victories for personal problems. In other words, we are not pursuing God to be blessed for our own sakes. But rather, through our blessings, we truly become the light and salt of the earth. Through our victories, we would become an open epistle read of all men about how good our God is, so that the world might take notice and be saved. This is the message of Isaiah 60:1-3:

> Arise, shine; for your light has come! And the glory of the Lord is risen upon you. For behold, the darkness shall cover the earth, and deep darkness the people; but the Lord will arise over you, and His glory will be seen upon you. The Gentiles shall come to your light, and kings to the brightness of your rising.

Should we not then arise and shine? Or are we going to miss our opportunity as Israel did in the days of Christ, and receive from Him the same lamentation as they did?

> If you had known, even you, especially in this your day, the things *that make* for your peace! But now they are hidden from your eyes…because you did not know the time of your visitation (Luke 19:41-44).

The choice, as always, is ours to make:

> I have set before you life and death, blessing and cursing; therefore choose life, that both you and your descendants may live; that you may love the Lord your God, that you may obey His voice, and that you may cling to Him, for He *is* your life and the length of

your days; and that you may dwell in the land which the Lord swore to your fathers... (Deut. 30:19-20)

CHAPTER 12

A WORD OF CAUTION: We Walk by Faith and Not by Sight

If you have understood the need to seek God and to hear His word, I know you would be eager to hear the voice of God from now on. But let me remind you that faith is required in this quest.

When we read the Bible from chapter to chapter, it is not always immediately obvious how long it took Abraham, for instance, to hear from God from one period to the next. We should not assume that, when we are friends with God, we are going to hear a fresh word from Him everyday about every turn we have to take. If we think like that we would be setting ourselves for disappointment, because that is not the way of God.

God does not micro-manage any thing He created. Rather, He empowers His creation to fulfill its set purpose (see, for instance, Genesis 1: 11, 22, 28). That was His way from the beginning, and that is still His way today.

Walking by faith is a creative spiritual skill that God expects us to develop over time. Faith is not an after-thought principle God instituted when man sinned, and needed a savior. Rather, faith will always be the only way we can relate to God.

If we ever came to the place where we knew all there was to know about God, then faith would become unnecessary, because we would know for sure the outcome of each step we take. However, to the extent that we shall never come to the point of knowing all there is to know about God because of His infinite capacity, we are always going to need faith to relate to God.

The reason it is vital we walk only by faith is that, as we walk with God, we are going to run into seasons, where it appears God is silent, and not responding to any of our prayers. Those are tricky times, when the enemy tries to cause much confusion in the mind of the believer. But if we can remember the unfailing love of God and all His faithful promises, we can still trust Him even in the midst of or our darkest hour. Let us adopt David's posture in such circumstance: *"Yea, though I walk through the valley of the shadow of death, I will fear no evil"* (Psalm 23:4).

When we run into darkness, we should continue to walk by what we already know of God. We should not light our own fires to make a way for ourselves, as Isaiah 50:11 warns us not to do. We are only accountable for what Gold has revealed to us.

The Bible says there are secret things of God that He has not yet revealed to anyone else, and those things, the Bible also says, belong to God (see Deuteronomy 29:29). Sometimes, it is during those night seasons in our lives that God reveals to us some of those secrets.

What Is In A Name?

Talking about secret things yet to be revealed, do you know Jesus has another name that no one knows at this present time? Well in Revelation 3:12 Jesus promises to write on those who would overcome in the Philadelphia Church His *New Name*.

Without getting too far into another subject, let me say that a *name* in the spirit implies authority, potential or purpose. So when Jesus reveals that, in his name, believers would do miracles, He did not mean we should merely preface our prayers with the phrase, "in Jesus' name", as we so often do. He meant rather that we would have his authority to do the same things he did.

For instance, Jesus said he did all his works in the name of the Father (see John 10:25), but we never hear Jesus using the words, "in the name of my Father" before he performed any miracle. Certainly, there is nothing wrong declaring in whose authority we do the things Jesus commanded us to do. In fact, Philippians 2:9-11 says that God has exalted Jesus to such an authority that, at his name, every knee would bow to his lordship.

Nevertheless, we caution against the use of Jesus' name as a magical incantation to effect things in the spirit. Let us rather understand, whether we say it loudly or not, that whatever we do as believers, we aught to do it in the authority of Jesus.

So when Jesus says in Revelations 3:12 that he would reveal his *new name* to those who would overcome, it implies that there are certain dimensions of Christ' authority that no one knows at this time. That also means believers who overcome will be given special authority to do things they cannot imagine in this present time.

The Scriptures say that when Christ appears, we shall see Him as He is, but '*as He is*' depends on what we know of Him presently. He will then take some of us into another dimension, and expand our knowledge of Him. This is not the place to fully expound this truth, but I hope you get the point.

It is evident, therefore, what God's intention was when He made animals of all kinds, and brought them to Adam to *name* them (Genesis 2:19). Adam had to name the animals because God had given him the dominion over the earth. Therefore, God was signifying to Adam that the details of what happens in the earth were Adam's responsibility.

Notice that Adam did not ask God what each animal should be called. Adam could have said something like: "Well, Lord, since you made these animals, you alone would know what they are, so tell me, and I will name them exactly as you want me to."

Typically that is how many of us understand our relationship with God to be: "God we know what your will is, but supply us with all the details about your will, so we can do something with it." If we continue to think like that, then we will forever be waiting to do the will of God, because that is not the way of God, as we have already explained throughout this book.

The revelation in Adam naming the animals is found in the statement:

> Out of the ground the Lord God formed every beast of the field and every bird of the air, and brought them to Adam to see what he would call them. **And whatever Adam called each living creature, that was its name** (Genesis 2:19 – emphasis added)

First, God wanted to see what Adam would call what He (God) had created. In the same way, God comes to us, and presents us with His purpose or will for us to see how we would accomplish and establish it in the earth. This should be the fun part for both God and man. God wants us to use our creativity to fulfill His will in the earth.

Unfortunately, for many of God's children, the lack of complete information has been the scariest part in our faith walk. We are so much used to a three-dimensional world, that anything that is not certain in our view causes consternation. But that is exactly where the comfort of the Holy Spirit comes in. He is here to direct our paths, as promised in Proverbs 3, and to guide us with His eye, as promised in Psalm 32. If we would veer off course, the Holy Spirit will rein us in, as long as we are depending on Him by acknowledging Him in our ways.

Secondly, the Scripture above says that, *"Whatever Adam called each living creature, that was its name."* So whatever name we assign to the purpose God reveals to us that is exactly how that purpose will turn out to be. Let us say that in another way: How far we can see our purpose in God is exactly what strength we will receive to accomplish that purpose. This is the law of faith: *"as you believed, so let it be done for you" (see Matthew 8:13* and also in Matthew 9:29).

All the above is to say that, God hardly gives the full details to man about anything He wants man to accomplish in the earth. I believe this is the fun part of God bringing us into His family by making us in His image and likeness. As we renew our mind, and come to know God, we would have what Paul describes as the 'mind of Christ' — We would begin to think like Christ thinks. In that state, our creativity, coming out of our renewed mind, will only produce results that mirror the perfect will of God.

This means, when God reveals His purpose to us, He wants us to use our creativity to establish that purpose in the earth. So how much of God's kingdom we are able to establish in the earth depends on what we are able to see by faith what the will of God is. So if the kingdom of God is not being established as fast as we would want to see, then the problem lies with our faith and not God's incapacity or reluctance.

Remember in earlier chapters, we showed how Jesus had such a close relationship with God he knew what to do and when to do it according to the will of God. Therefore, when Jesus said he did everything as the Father did, it did not mean the Father spoke to him about every detail for him to do His will. Instead, Jesus' knowledge of God's way allowed him to act in accordance with God's will.

We also noticed that, as a result of his close intimacy with the Father, Jesus did not need to pray to the Father to perform a miracle. He just commanded and it was done, because the Father had given him authority to do what he had to do. It is this intimacy that God wants to nurture in us, so that we will become like those mature folks who Hebrews 5:14 describes as:

> …Those who are mature, who have trained them-
> selves to recognize the difference between right and
> wrong and then do what is right (NLT).

This is the reason for Psalm 32:8, 9 with which we are already familiar, but we quote here again to refresh our memory of the salient points:

> I will instruct you and teach you in the way you
> should go; I will guide you with My eye. **Do not
> be like the horse or like the mule, which have no
> understanding, which must be harnessed with
> bit and bridle, else they will not come near you**
> (emphasis added).

So let us simply say that faith is the way for us to go. And in walking by faith, we are walking in uncertainty of outcomes. Faith therefore entails risks and an enormous amount of trust in an invincible God.

Just how would you deal with a word like this: *"Get out of your country, from your family into a land **I will show you?**"* How do you leave everything you have, to go to a place you do not even know yet? But that was exactly the word on which Abraham started his journey.

Faith is a risky business, and that is why so many of us are afraid to walk by faith. Nevertheless, let us pursue God with the faith He has measured to us at this time, and as we become faithful with what He gave us, we shall discover promotion unto a higher level of faith and glory.

Victory Belongs to Originals and not Copycats

We made it clear at the beginning of this book that how far we go in God will depend on our faith and the unique purpose God has ordained for each of us to accomplish in the earth. That is why it is imperative that we discover and experience God for ourselves, according to our unique personalities and dispositions.

Trying to copy from the testimonies of others specific actions or dispositions that earned them those testimonies will only lead to frustration. In fact, doing specific things to earn specific results without the Spirit of God is what dead religion is about.

Instead, let us be steadfast and consistent in the things we are already assured of through our own walk with God. And God, in His infinite wisdom, will add to us as He sees fit.

Even if nothing we discussed in this book impressed you at all, you can still take this one resolve with you: never accept an unanswered prayer as a matter of course. Be violent in the spirit, and pound on the gates of Heaven until God answers one way or the other. Why? Because, the stubborn problem facing you today might just be only one *word of God* away from leaving you permanently!

Printed in the United States
77304LV00003B/139-999

9 781597 816137